The
Retirement
Guide

The
Retirement
Guide

A Comprehensive Handbook on Aging,
Retirement, Caregiving and Health:
How to Plan and Pay for it

Michael S. Midlam
Jill O'Donnell,
Graham McWaters
and John A. Page

INSOMNIAC PRESS

Cover and interior design by Marijke Friesen

Library and Archives Canada Cataloguing in Publication

O'Donnell, Jill, 1940-
The retirement guide : a comprehensive handbook on aging, retirement, caregiving and health : how to plan and pay for it / Jill O'Donnell, Graham McWaters, Michael S. Midlam, John A. Page.

Includes index.
ISBN 1-894663-79-9

1. Retirement income—United States—Planning. 2. Retirement—United States—Planning. I. McWaters, Graham, 1956- II. Page, John A., 1946- III. Title.

HQ1063.2.U6O36 2004   332.024'01   C2004-903947-4

The publisher gratefully acknowledges the support of the Canada Council, the Ontario Arts Council and the Department of Canadian Heritage through the Book Publishing Industry Development Program.

Printed and bound in Canada

Insomniac Press
192 Spadina Avenue, Suite 403
Toronto, Ontario, Canada, M5T 2C2
www.insomniacpress.com

THE CANADA COUNCIL | LE CONSEIL DES ARTS
FOR THE ARTS | DU CANADA
SINCE 1957 | DEPUIS 1957

ONTARIO ARTS COUNCIL
CONSEIL DES ARTS DE L'ONTARIO

DISCLAIMER

The material in this book is provided for general information and is subject to change without notice. Every effort has been made to compile this material from reliable sources. This material is not intended to provide, and should not be construed as providing individual financial, investment, tax, legal, accounting, or medical advice. If legal advice or other expert assistance is required, the services of a qualified professional should be sought.

Every effort has been made to use current information as of the date of publication.

Commissions, trailing commissions, management fees, and expenses may all be associated with mutual fund investments. The indicated rates of return are the historical annual compounded total returns including changes in unit/share value and reinvestment of all distributions/dividends. They do not take into account sales, redemption, distribution or optional charges or income taxes payable by any security holder that would have reduced returns. Mutual funds are not guaranteed, their values change frequently and past performance may not be repeated. Please read the prospectus and consult a financial advisor before investing.

TABLE OF CONTENTS

INTRODUCTION 11

Part I: Life Planning

1 GROWING OLDER **19**
Personal Responsibility, Attitude, Relationships, Your Inner Self

2 YOUR LIFE PLAN **25**
Who Are You?, Reflecting on Your Life, Aiming for Balance, Following
Your Dreams, Prioritizing, Writing Your Mission Statement, Setting
Goals, Being Well Informed, Analyzing Your Situation, Devising Your
Strategy, Putting Your Plan into Action

3 BODY AND MIND **39**
Staying Healthy, Keeping Active, Eating Properly, Practicing
Moderation, Seeing Your Doctor, Managing Stress, Staying Safe and
Secure, Using Your Mind, Companionship, Appearance, Learning,
Working, Sharing

4 WHERE WILL YOU HANG YOUR HAT? **51**
Making the Right Choice, Staying in Your Own Home, Remaining
Independent, Adapting Your House, Some Factors for Homeowners to
Consider, Buying a Condominium, Continuing Care Retirement
Communities, Renting an Apartment or Condominium, Senior's
Communities, Retirement Homes, Finding the Right Fit, Moving in
with Family, Long-Term Care Facilities, Planning the Move

5 THE TIES THAT BIND **67**
Parent–Child Relationships, Communicating across Generations,
Planning Together, Communicating With Family Members, Factors That
Can Impair Communication, Selling the Family Home, Bequests and
Legacies, Second Marriages and New Relationships, Financial Problems,
Living with Adult Children, Differences in Attitudes and Beliefs

6 PUTTING YOUR LEGAL HOUSE IN ORDER **81**
Role of Professionals, Types of Powers of Attorney, Living Wills or Directives, Consent to Treatment, Adult Guardianship, Compensation, Wills and Trusts, Mental Capacity, Selecting an Executor: Factors to Consider, Compensation for Estate Administration, Bequests and Legacies, Family Law Issues, Prenuptial Agreements, Family Law Obligations

7 THE FINAL EXIT **95**
Cremation, After Cremation, Earth Burial, Burial Vault, Caskets and Containers, Funeral Service, Memorial Service, Location of the Service, Church Funeral, Graveside Service, Funeral Home Chapel Service, Non-Religious Service, Pre-Planning Your Funeral, Funeral Trust

Part II: Caregiving

8 BEING A CAREGIVER **109**
Are You Equipped for Caregiving?, Attitudes, Being Partners, Responsibilities, Being Informed, Making Decisions, Workplace Concerns, Stress, Feelings Related to Caregiving, Coping with Anger and Frustration, Family Involvement, Taking Care of Yourself

9 PROVIDING CARE **125**
Identifying Age-Related Changes, How to Cope, Assessing Needs, Informal Support Systems, Formal Support Systems, Locating Support Services, Local Community Information Center, Government Services, Telephone Book & Yellow Pages, Internet, Consulting Services, Hiring Staff, Senior Abuse, Problem Solving, Loneliness, Finding a New Home, Dealing with Doctors, Lawyers, and Financial Advisors, Driving, Creating a Safe Environment, Distance Caregiving, What is a Geriatric Care Manager, Who needs a Geriatric Care Manager

10 COPING WITH DEMENTIA **147**
Causes and Development, Diagnosing Dementia, Progressive Changes to Expect, Communication, Aggressive Behavior, Hygiene,

Meal Times, Wandering, Nighttime Concerns, Safety Measures, Legal Matters, Activities for Seniors with Dementia, Music and Dance, Photographs, Walking, Reading

Part III: Financial Planning

11 WHY PLAN? **161**
Objectives of Financial Planning, Why People Don't Plan Financially

12 YOUR FINANCIAL PLAN **169**
Principles of Financial Planning, The Role of a Financial Advisor, Steps in Financial Planning, 1. Goals and Objectives, 2. Information, 3. Analysis, 4. Financial Strategy, 5. Action Plan, 6. Decisions for Action, Review and Update

13 BOOSTING THE BOTTOM LINE **183**
Principles of Cash Management, Minimizing the Cost of Your Chosen Lifestyle, Avoid Non-Deductible Debt, Maximizing After-Tax Discretionary Income, Deduct, Defer, Diminish, Divide

14 MAKING YOUR MONEY GROW **195**
Types of Investment, Debt (Fixed-Income) Investments, Equity Investments, Risk, Inflation, Variability, Comparing the Risks, Other Components of Risk, Managing Risk and Prospering, Diversification, Ways to Diversify, Maintaining a Model Asset Allocation, Contrarian Investment Approach, Due Diligence, Investment Management Points to Remember

15 PROTECTING YOURSELF AND YOUR FAMILY **209**
Principles of Risk Management, What Are the Risks?, Disability, Critical Illness, Need for Long-Term Care, Premature Death, Are You Covered?, Capital Analysis in the Event of Death, Capital Analysis in the Event of Need for Long-Term Care

16 PLANNING YOUR ESTATE **227**
Common Goals of Estate Planning, Estate Planning in General

17 CHOOSING A FINANCIAL ADVISOR 235
Professional Qualifications, Questions You Should Ask, How Are
Financial Advisors Paid?, Fee-Only Financial Planners, Commission-
Based Financial Planners, Fee-Based Financial Planners, Wrap
Accounts

18 OVERCOMING POSSIBLE PROBLEMS 247
Fear of Equities, Annuities, Reverse Mortgages, Benefits and
Drawbacks, Reverse Mortgages: Benefits and Drawbacks, Financial
Independence Deficit, Family Dynamics

APPENDIX A: TYPES OF INSURANCE 263
Disability Insurance, Life Insurance

APPENDIX B: PREPARING TO MEET YOUR ADVISORS 269
Your Financial Advisor, Your Estate-Planning Advisor, Your Lawyer,
Your Executor

APPENDIX C: INTERVIEWING A FINANCIAL ADVISOR 293

INDEX 298

Introduction

Get ready…Get set…Here comes tomorrow!

By the year 2011, the first baby boomers will reach 65. Over the coming decades, those born between 1946 and 1965 will dominate and transform society, as they have at each stage of their lives. Elderboomers will reshape the way we view aging—from clothing trends to lifestyles. Today's 65-year-olds are fit and active. Many are still productively employed; others are taking university courses, enjoying travel, embarking on new relationships, or pursuing challenging new interests.

Seniors already constitute the fastest growing segment of the population in the United States. In 2003 there were 77,702,865 baby boomers aged 39 - 57 representing 27.5% of the US population. Baby boomers born between 1946 - 1965 will begin retiring in 2011, representing over 77 million in the US, more than a quarter of the nation's population. With a wealthier, healthier, aging society, demands for attention to seniors' issues will grow. Our government will be forced to listen to this group, which will play a significant role in changing laws and policies that have an impact on the environment, health, social issues, schooling (because of grandchildren), and housing.

Our life spans are increasing and, along with them, the options for how we will spend our later years. How we choose to live our lives is dependent on many things—our education, the kind of work we do, how much we earn; our personal experiences and beliefs; how we spend our leisure time; and our relationships with others—all our wants, needs, and desires. Together these factors create our quality of life.

What is your vision for your future? How do you perceive aging? How do you hope to spend your final years? Whether you are in your 30s, 60s, or 90s, whether you feel well-prepared, not prepared, or had good plans that have now been upset, this book is designed to help you plan strategically to make your future all you want it to be.

Life Planning

The first step is to know what you really want. In the opening section of this book, you'll learn how to determine what is most important to you and how to create a strategic Life Plan to achieve your goals.

Your health, how you wish to spend your time, and where you will live, are all key issues to consider in your planning. Up-to-date information on each is provided to help you look ahead.

Aging is a family affair. But family communication is not always easy. A chapter on family issues includes strategies for improving communication and coping with common problems.

You want to ensure your wishes continue to be met as you age. The chapter on legal responsibilities describes writing a will and setting up Powers of Attorney—decisions that are always wise to make earlier rather than later. The final chapter in this section outlines funeral options.

The guiding principle of this book is: *We are each responsible for our own lives and for all entrusted to us; we are responsible for our own living, aging, and dying, and for our relationships with others.* This means that you resolve to be proactive, to plan for your future, for the life and lifestyle you hope to have, and that you refuse to let anyone else control how you deal with the important questions in your own life. While others may enlighten you by the information and examples they provide, you do not want, if you can help it, to be deprived of the responsibilities that are yours.

Caregiving

How best to care for aging parents, who are also living longer, is one of the biggest questions facing the boomer generation. It is becoming more critical for families to plan together for this financial responsibility, yet few are prepared for it. Some will find themselves dependent on their own children, because they did not foresee the financial ramifications of caring for their elderly parents. As well as financial demands, caregiving involves many other challenges. The second section of this book deals with the day-to-day problems caregivers may face. It describes how to determine when care is needed, solve common caregiving dilemmas, including distance caregiving, improving communication, and coping with relatives who suffer from dementia. It also provides strategies caregivers can use to help take care of themselves.

Financial Planning

Developing a financial plan, and managing it with the assistance of a knowledgeable financial professional, can help you live a happy and secure life. Increasing your net worth and reducing taxes should be a primary goal. Protecting your assets from unusual and unfavorable circumstances should be part of your plan. Establishing an estate plan today is a must.

When you don't feel well, you go to a doctor; when you have a toothache, you go to a dentist; when you have legal issues, you consult a lawyer. When you want to plan and manage your finances for a secure and happy future, it's wise to work with a financial professional. The needs of each individual are quite different when it comes to financial planning. Each person has a unique set of circumstances that make them different from others. Creating a customized plan to meet your circumstances is the goal of a financial professional. In this section, you'll find out why people often don't plan, how the financial planning process works, what a financial professional can do for you, and how to select one who suits your needs.

Despite the important consequences for the rest of our well being, it's surprising how few hours many of us are willing to devote to the purpose of improving our financial health. In many cases, far more time is spent deciding what new car to buy, or which vacation destination to choose, than on making a well thought out choice for our investments. Investing can be easy and it can also be difficult. Working with a financial professional who understands your needs as well as your risk tolerance, will make it easier for you to sleep at night. In this section, you'll find out how to spread your risk by not putting all your eggs in one basket, aiming for long-term rather than short-term gains, minimizing taxation, and balancing your portfolio to meet your current and future needs.

Insurance is an overlooked area in many people's lives. Will your family have sufficient funds to maintain a comfortable lifestyle should you die prematurely? Will your estate be able to manage the probate taxes on their inheritance? These are just a few questions you need to answer as you review your insurance requirements. This section provides information to help you customize the insurance component of your financial plan.

If your income is low, or you don't have a comfortable investment portfolio to draw from in the later years of your life, some additional cash flow may be required to meet your standard of living. If you own real estate, there may be opportunities available to you that you are not aware of. Your real estate may be used to improve cash flow now and/or in the future.

Finally, when you die, will those you love be left struggling with debts, or reduced legacies, due to inadequate estate planning? Using the estate planning checklist and working with your financial advisor, you can ensure that you end your life as well as you lived it.

Part I
Life Planning

1

Growing Older

When you think about aging—its processes, challenges, and opportunities—what concerns you the most? Maintaining control of your life as you age and your capacities diminish? Being financially secure? Staying healthy and involved with life? Finding meaning in life? In this book, you'll learn how to develop a life plan and financial plan to help meet your goals. Considering what is most important to you in life can help you gain insights that will lead to wise decisions.

What does it mean to grow old? What does it mean for you and for those you love? How can you help one another traverse the final stages of life with security rather than anxiety, acceptance rather than rejection, courage and anticipation instead of fear and loathing, integrity and dignity rather then disintegration and dehumanization, completion and hope, not disorder and despair?

Personal Responsibility

Let's look at some situations that older people face. Already you may have identified circumstances you wish to avoid as well as those in which you would prefer to find yourself. You want to have as much control as possible over your future.

You want to think ahead, clarify your intentions, and make responsible decisions about the future management of all your affairs—while you are still competent to do so. You want to be sure that, as far as possible, decisions that may be made someday on your behalf are in essential agreement with what you would have decided yourself.

Personal responsibility can become, or continue to be, a sustaining and empowering principle in your own life with each responsible decision you make, either alone or with others. And the way you care for yourself will largely determine your ability to care for others.

Attitude

An optimistic attitude is one of the keys to happiness—a positive attitude leads to positive results. Being optimistic means recognizing that most problems are temporary—things can change for the better. It means focusing on specific problems, rather than giving up and letting life unravel when one thread snaps. Optimists expect life to go well and do not blame themselves or others when it does not. They know that it is not so much what happens to them, but how they think about it—and what they decide to do about it—that determines how they feel.

If you are blessed with good health and meaningful relationships, if you have beliefs and values that motivate and sustain you, you may feel satisfaction and hope for the future. You may feel you have been accumulating the resources and wisdom to cope with your own aging. You may be able to keep facing each new day and each fresh or continuing challenge with confidence, optimism, energy, and ambition.

But sometimes, in the face of major setbacks, optimism can fail. What then? Can you graciously bear your own extended or permanent illness? Imagine having to look after someone else if that condition becomes a confining burden and frustration for you, the caregiver? What if the power of choice is no longer exclusively yours, or worse, practically non-existent? What if life falls in on you, and meaning and purpose desert you? What can help you endure, and even vanquish, the worst you have to go through?

It takes a great deal of courage to survive and even thrive in the face of adversities. It can be a terrible shock to your sense of identity and dignity to be forced to admit that you are no longer able to work, or drive a car, or even feed and clean yourself.

How often have you known people, perhaps one of your loved ones, to survive extreme difficulties with optimism, grace, and good humor? Such an attitude takes both courage and willpower. But what inspires it? For most, it is a sense of meaning and purpose—having something worth fighting and living for. A sense of meaning and purpose can contribute to the healing of body, mind, and spirit.

David was diagnosed with cancer when he was just 55 years old. It was in his bones, liver, lymph nodes, and brain. He had an incredible will to live and a strong belief in a higher being. After two years of chemotherapy, he returned to his oncologist, who was completely taken aback—David was in total remission. Today, he is 76 years old, suffering some of the slings and arrows of aging, but the cancer is still in remission. 'Believe in yourself' was his credo and, for him, it worked.

Relationships

Life is a journey enriched by companionship. No one really wants to venture along their journey completely alone.

One of the most helpful ways to understand your value and purpose can be through the exploration of your interpersonal relationships. To love and be loved is an essential part of being human. Remember the essential principle of human relationships: *Treat others the way you would like them to treat you.* This principle is shared, in some form, by all the great religions—Christianity, Judaism, Islam, Confucianism, Hinduism, and Buddhism—and is known as the Golden Rule. The character of your daily living and the quality of your life depend directly on the values and attitudes that govern how you relate to others and how they relate to you.

Your Inner Self

As you age, you mature, and grow wiser. You have experience that makes dealing with challenges easier, and you have accumulated knowledge that enables you to learn about and appreciate life. You have a clearer perspective on what's really important to you; you know yourself better.

As you age, you will likely find yourself beginning to think more often about what you actually do believe and why. Some of the questions you ask yourself may be ones you have not thought about before. Others, you may have been struggling with as long as you can remember. Still others, you may have been avoiding.

When asked what he found most difficult to understand, a worldly wise businessman replied: "I think I can figure most things out for myself, but these baffle me: the divine spirit, electricity, and my teenage children!"

The hard questions children ask themselves—Who am I? Where did I come from? Why am I here?—persist throughout life. Fundamental anxieties—about death and non-being, meaninglessness, what you may or may not have done—often become more acute with age. Gradually or suddenly, you realize that the longer you live, the sooner you are going to die. These anxieties are part of what it means to exist as a human being.

Have you ever suffered with any of them? Or wondered whether someone whom you care for might be experiencing them? These anxieties can threaten your sense of security and identity. How much of what happens to me, you may ask, is within my personal control? How can I, how should I, respond to life's contingencies and my approaching end? Who or what assures me that who I am or what I do is significant?

Life and its meaning, the world and the universe, are infinitely complex. Some find answers and insight in the sacred texts of their faith. You may glimpse eternal truths while reflecting upon your life experience. Many find knowledge and wisdom in the insights of philosophers and scholars, sages and prophets. Poems, music, and songs that catch your imagination or touch your heart, people you are close to—all that adds quality and value to your life can help mirror your inner self and illuminate life's meaning.

Reviewing your life, regularly, responsibly, and honestly, will help you understand where you have come from and what you have been doing with your life so far, and to appreciate some of the problems and potential of your future. Your experiences, the people you know, and your beliefs can all stimulate your reflections. They can help you see yourself more clearly, and be more objective about your situation and circumstances. They may remind you of your good fortune; they may also increase your anxieties. They can help you recognize your strengths and weaknesses. When you attend to what they reveal to you, they can help you make realistic decisions, act courageously, and deal responsibly with whatever lies ahead.

You know there is much about your future, and that of those whom you love, that you cannot hope to foresee accurately. Positively, however, you recognize that there are many eventualities—declining vigor or health, changes in career and residence, financial concerns, loss of friends and relatives, and death—that you must meet sooner or later. It makes sense to learn as much as you can, while you can, so you are better equipped to make the right decisions.

Acknowledge the reality of your aging. Persevere, learn from any mistakes or misadventures. Recognize that it is better to have others to grow old with, than to have to do it alone.

Would you really want to live forever? Probably not. But almost everyone would like his or her life to last longer. Small, unimportant things can too easily fill up a day. Try to spend more time on the things that really matter to you.

2

Your Life Plan

If someone were to ask you if you have a life plan, how would you respond? Where do you want to be in 10, 20, 30, or even 60 years? Where do you want to be tomorrow? You have goals you hope to achieve. You want to be sure you have sufficient means to meet your needs, not just now, but in the future. But what about those concerns that lie beyond the realm of finances? What makes your life full, and meaningful? What is most important to you?

The life-planning process is very personal. It focuses on non-financial goals such as health, personal fulfillment, and family involvement, without losing sight of financial goals and the need to save and invest for a secure future. Many financial professionals can guide you through the maze of options available and help you select those that best suit your needs. But first, you need to define your vision for your life and set some personal goals, the first steps in developing your own strategic life plan, an action plan that will help put you where you want to be tomorrow.

Who Are You?

What is the vision you have for your life? A life vision is not a forecast of what the future holds; rather it looks into the future and assembles a picture of what could be. It results from a process of observing yourself, thinking and dreaming about your life, and learning about and planning for the future. Your vision will be your compass as you chart your life journey. It will help you stay on course, measure how far you've gone, and persevere in the face of obstacles or setbacks. The first step in successful planning is to write a mission statement that captures your vision.

Reflecting on Your Life

Ask yourself: Who am I, and what is most important to me? What motivates me? What personal values are key to me?

What has made you feel most secure, or most challenged? With whom have you felt most loved or esteemed? Where have you experienced the greatest sense of belonging? When did you feel you were most valued for who you are? In what situations were you most able to use your abilities or talents, or pursue your greatest interests in a satisfying way?

Before writing your mission statement, take time to reflect on these questions. Thinking about significant people, places, and events in your life, and the impact they've had on you, can also be helpful. For each decade of your life, list the people and things that had the most meaning for you, those you most enjoyed, and those you did not. Keep an open mind. You may discover that some things you once didn't like or enjoy, are what you want to try to do now.

Reflect on the past with a view to the future. Once you have written down your thoughts, look for elements—particular people, places, or events—that keep recurring. These can be clues to who you are and what really matters to you.

Important People, Places, and Events

In my teens _____

_____

In my 20s_____

_____

In my 30s_____

_____

In my 40s_____

_____

In my 50s_____

_____

In my 60s_____

_____

In my 70s_____

_____

In my 80s_____

_____

Aiming for Balance

Does your life feel well balanced? You know you need balance in your day-to-day life, but things can easily spin out of control. This creates stress, which can play havoc with your health and outlook. Look at your current situation and try to identify where changes need to be made to make your life more balanced.

Often, people put so much energy into one aspect of their life—parenthood, a personal relationship, their career, caregiving—that they forget to look at the whole picture. But children grow up and leave home, friends can move far away, and careers often end at retirement. And you can only care effectively for someone else when you also care for yourself. Life planning can help you recognize when you are overextended and see when it is time to change direction and head toward new horizons that will give new meaning to your life.

As you review your life, you may remember, with justifiable pride, your successes. On the other hand, there may be recollections of failures that you need to acknowledge, at least to yourself, with the realization that, at times, whether you won or lost, you didn't always measure up as well as you wish you had. Are there areas of your life that you're not comfortable with, perhaps involving unresolved issues in your past? Are these situations that you might yet remedy or even rectify? Ask yourself: What can I do about this now? What do I want to do? An argument may have broken a valued long-term relationship, to your regret. Perhaps you would now like to contact that person.

Once you start to resolve old issues, you'll be surprised at how much more energy you have for the things you want to accomplish.

Following Your Dreams

Dreams do come true. What do you dream about doing that you haven't explored? Putting a plan together means realizing those dreams.

> When they were in their 70s, Rose took up belly dancing, Hanna enrolled in a tap-dancing class, and Liliana took an extended trip to the Far East. They had always dreamed of doing these things, but had always put their families' needs before their own.

Not everyone has the talent and commitment to be a concert pianist, but learning to play the piano is possible at any age. It just takes desire and discipline. How many people know Grandma Moses' real name? As the wife of a farmer, Anna May Robertson Moses placed her husband and family's needs first. She didn't gain renown as an artist until she was in her 70s, but it's a good bet that her dream was formulated long before.

So, what makes you happy, and what, in the larger scheme of things, would you like to change?

What I'm Happy With and What I Want to Change

Personal relationships (family, friends, lovers)

I am happy with_____

_____

I want to change _____

_____

Home

I am happy with_____

_____

I want to change _____

_____

Health

I am happy with_____

_____

I want to change _____

_____

Education and career (formal/informal, achievements, accomplishments)

I am happy with_____

_____

I want to change _____

_____

Financial (income, home ownership, assets, acquisitions)

I am happy with_____

_____

I want to change _____

_____

Community self (volunteering, social/service clubs, religious organizations)

I am happy with_____

_____

I want to change _____

_____

Leisure self (recreation, entertainment, travel)

I am happy with_____

_____

I want to change _____

_____

Inner self (creative, intellectual, spiritual)

I am happy with_____

_____

I want to change _____

_____

Prioritizing

To focus your vision, you need to prioritize. From the lists you've made, pick those items that are most meaningful to you and have the strongest bearing on your future. Ask yourself which best reflect your deepest values and aspirations—what you want most out of life.

Writing Your Mission Statement

In writing your mission statement, aim for a few, simple sentences, ones you'll easily be able to remember.

Andrew, an 84-year-old retired pharmacist who loved spending time in his garden and visiting friends, wrote, "I want to enjoy all the days that are left to the best of my ability."

Describe what you want to achieve, rather than how you'll do it. The following mission statement encapsulates a life vision that could be actualized in many ways.

> Michelle, a 40-year-old homemaker, wrote, "To support my children as they grow and my parents as they age, to be a good friend, to contribute to my community, and to live close to nature."

Even if you're sure you know what you want to achieve and how best to do it, try to frame your statement to allow for other possible approaches.

> Joshua, in his 30s, wrote: "To be promoted to vice-president, to write a best-selling novel, and to own a villa in Spain." He did meet his goals of career satisfaction, artistic expression, and a comfortable retreat, but it turned out to be as the owner of a literary publishing company based in a beautiful little town.

On the other hand, don't be too general. "I want to make more money" could mean many things. You might desire more money to retire earlier or more comfortably, have a larger home, better assist your children or grandchildren, travel, or contribute more to causes you care about. Try to describe specific ends, without being too specific about how they might be achieved.

My personal mission statement for my life plan is:

_____

_____

_____

_____

_____

_____

Setting Goals

The vision you have articulated gives you a framework for determining specific objectives. Use the chart below to start to set your goals. Be realistic. Be specific. Focus on the things that mean the most to you. Much about life is unpredictable, and you'll want to revisit and re-evaluate your goals frequently, and to refine them as your needs or circumstances change.

Determine specifically what each goal is meant to achieve. Personal goals are quite different from social or leisure goals, just as educational goals are different from career goals, though they may be related. Financial goals are also a separate category, although some of your other goals will depend on achieving your financial goals. In each category, separate *short-term*, *intermediate*, and *long-term* goals. Set timelines for when you would like to achieve each objective. Writing down your goals will help you to stay focused on your plan and make it easier to review your progress.

Go back and review what you've written regarding what has meant the most to you, what you are happiest about, and the things you want to change. Personal goals can be as simple as *meeting at least one new person a month* or *joining a social club where you might find the perfect mate.*

A short-term goal for you may be *to make certain your children are receiving the best education available to them.* Your long-term goals could include a view of how you want to live out your later years. If you plan to retire at 55, and expect to be financially independent by then, you may envision yourself living on a houseboat in the Caribbean. You may think of moving to a retirement community where you can participate in the recreational activities you most enjoy. You may not see yourself retiring. You may expect to need to work to earn an income throughout your life; or, you may see yourself moving into a new and exciting role in your 50s, 60s—even 70s or 80s—doing something you always wanted to do.

With so many corporations and organizations downsizing, more people are becoming entrepreneurs. You might consider setting this as your new goal.

To get away for a weekend could be a short-term goal. Taking a vacation or a sabbatical from work, can be refreshing. In the longer term, you might aim to save for a trip to a far-off country.

Another short-term goal might be to volunteer a few hours a month. This could be the first step toward a long-term goal of working at a senior level in a not-for-profit organization whose goals you are committed to.

How you set financial goals will depend on your age, background, experience, and expectations of life in general. Perhaps you've contributed to retirement savings plans and also play the stock market. If you plan on becoming financially secure by a certain age, you have likely already set some goals and are working toward them. If you are just beginning your career, you should establish specific goals now.

Some of your goals may depend at least in part on another person, for example, a spouse or partner. If so, discuss these goals with him or her to be sure you're in sync. If partners don't take time to discuss their goals and personal desires together, they can invest time and energy only to find themselves at odds, or moving in completely different directions.

My Life Goals

Short-Term (within the next 2 years)

Personal relationships _____

Home _____

Health _____

Education and career _____

Financial_____

Community self_____

Leisure self _____

Inner self _____

Intermediate (within 2 to 10 years)

Personal relationships _____

Home _____

Health _____

Education and career _____

Financial_____

Community self_____

Leisure self _____

Inner self _____

Long-Term (beyond 10 years)

Personal relationships _____

Home _____

Health _____

Education and career _____

Financial_____

Community self_____

Leisure self _____

Inner self _____

Being Well Informed

You've thought about who you are and what's important to you. You've set some initial goals. Now you need to thoroughly analyze your situation.

Before beginning your analysis, gather together the information you'll need. Is research required before you can decide how best to meet some of your goals? Do you have up-to-date information?

To make an effective plan, you need to be well informed. This book contains a wealth of information on aging. It can help you see what different strategies might involve and introduce you to options and factors you might not have considered. You may wish to read the rest of this book before completing your life plan, or you may wish to draft your plan now, and then review it after you've considered the information in subsequent chapters.

Analyzing Your Situation

To decide how best to reach your goals, you first need a thorough understanding of your current situation. Consider the goals you've set, and ask yourself the following questions:

Are there special requirements—perhaps financial or educational—that you will need to meet first? Do you have other responsibilities that must be kept in mind? What might restrict or limit your ability to meet your goals?

What strengths do you bring to meeting a particular objective, and what weaknesses might you need to compensate for? What might be the most significant challenges, and the most time-sensitive opportunities?

Are your goals realistic? Do you have the time, money, or skills required? If not, can you get them? How? Or, how could your goals be changed to make them more achievable?

Devising Your Strategy

Strategic planning is a process followed by all well-run businesses and organizations. A strategic plan describes, in step-by-step detail, what needs to be accomplished, and when, if objectives are to be met.

When devising your strategy, consider and evaluate the most promising options for achieving your goals. There are usually many alternative paths to the same destination. You may find you need to make some compromises, or change your timeframe, to get to where you want to go. Plan for contingencies. Are there hidden assumptions that could undermine your plan? Is it relatively flexible? Life holds much that is unforeseen.

My Action Plan
Goals Strategies

Short-Term (within the next 2 years)

Personal relationships _____

_____

Home _____

_____

Health _____

_____

Education and career _____

_____

Financial_____

_____

Community self_____

_____

Leisure self _____

_____

Inner self _____

_____

Intermediate (within 2 to 10 years)

Personal relationships _____

Home _____

Health _____

Education and career _____

Financial_____

Community self_____

Leisure self _____

Inner self _____

Long-Term (beyond 10 years)

Personal relationships _____

Home _____

Health _____

Education and career _____

Financial_____

Community self_____

Leisure self _____

Inner self _____

Putting Your Plan into Action

You're ready to put your plan into action. By sticking to it, you'll be able to realize your dreams. Look at it often. Evaluate it regularly. What's turning out as planned? What isn't? What's been achieved so far? You may find it worthwhile to share your plan with a friend, colleague, or relative. They may remind you of aspects of yourself you haven't considered.

Update your plan regularly. Your needs or wants may change, as well as your abilities to achieve certain goals. Refer to your plan whenever there are significant changes in your life. Be open to revising your mission statement as well as your goals. Life is a continuum with occasional blips. If you're flexible and creative, you can always better your chances of success.

Think positively, plan well, and enjoy life. You only get one chance at it. Make it work!

3

Body
and Mind

Two little girls were playing house when one of them asked the other what she was going to be when she grew up. Without batting an eye, the second little girl replied, "Old."

Aging is inevitable, irreversible, universal and involves physical, psychological, and social change. Most people, regardless of age, are creatures of habit and, as such, resistant to change. Acceptance of the normal physical aging process, and the changes it brings, is not always easy. The manner in which you live your life affects how you age, and how you view your own aging determines how well you will adapt.

Aging is continuous from birth, but you may not really notice it until middle age. In your 40s, you may find yourself requiring reading glasses for smaller print. Arthritic changes may start occurring in your 50s. Your strength and stamina will slowly decline, along with your hearing. Your reaction times will also slow, your sleep patterns may change, and you may experience changes in your taste and appetite.

With advancing age, there is an increased risk of both acute and chronic health problems, such as diabetes, pulmonary and cardiac disease, and osteoporosis. Your cognition may begin to fail, and you may develop Alzheimer's or a form of dementia caused by strokes or Parkinson's disease. How these conditions are approached and treated can significantly impact the quality of life as you age. For most diseases, appropriate management can make it possible to continue living an active life. Today, preventive health care even extends to the reversal of many disease-promoting genetic tendencies and lifestyle patterns. Recent advances in the fields of genetics, nutrition, and hormonal replacement allow doctors to anticipate disease susceptibility and customize treatment plans to address the underlying causes.

Diet, exercise, and stress management all help to slow the process of aging, prevent disease, and optimize physical, mental, and emotional well-being. As you age, you may even become more fit and healthy, or as healthy, as when you were much younger. If you were a smoker or regularly drank too much coffee, alcohol, or soda pop, worked and played too hard, never got enough sleep, and never exercised much, and if you have now quit unhealthy habits and have started eating better, exercising, and getting the sleep you need, your biological age may now be younger.

Take a proactive and preventive approach to your health management. There's a tremendous amount you can do to stay healthy and fit as you age. Taking care of your health pays dividends at any age, not only in decreasing illness and increasing longevity, but also in creating more energy and enjoyment of life.

Staying Healthy

Keeping Active

Regular exercise slows aging. Participating in physical activity is arguably the single most important thing you can do to maintain good physical and mental health. Activities such as golf, bowling, bicycling, swimming, or walking are relatively undemanding, yet loaded with health benefits. Many seniors today, in their 60s, 70s, and 80s, are embarking on much more strenuous activities—jogging, marathon running, weightlifting, aerobic exercise, dance, and martial arts—just to feel good. Exercise improves reflexes, balance, and coordination. It increases energy levels, muscle tone, strength, and stamina. It can help you lose weight and improve your posture.

Explore what types of exercise are suitable for your level of fitness. Select an exercise program that you're comfortable with and that suits your schedule and level of motivation. Some sports are not suitable for brittle bones.

Whatever activity you choose, it must be one that you enjoy. The important thing is to get involved in some form of regular physical activity, then stick to it. When starting a new form of exercise, and particularly if you haven't been in the habit of regular exercise, always start slowly. Increase your activity level gradually. Make sure you have the proper equipment and clothing.

Should you lack the strength or endurance to complete a full class, of aerobics, or a martial art, ask the instructor whether you can participate in part of the class.

Aim to exercise briskly for at least 15 to 20 minutes three times a week. You'll look better and feel better. If you're already into fitness, keep it up! If not, get into it!

Eating Properly

Many health problems stem from, or are exacerbated by, poor nutrition. More emphasis needs to be placed on a well-balanced diet that includes the four food groups: 1) milk and milk products, 2) meat, chicken, fish and alternatives, 3) breads and cereals (whole grains), and 4) fruits and vegetables. Even many health care professionals ignore the need for proper nutrition.

Learn how nutritional needs change as you age. Women need more calcium. Everyone should eat less sodium, sugar, and fat. Make certain you eat plenty of fresh fruits and vegetables, cereals and grains. Eat less red meat by using alternatives such as fish or chicken. Drink at least 6 to 8 glasses of water daily. Vitamins, minerals, antioxidants, and other micronutrients are also critical to health, and for some, supplements may be necessary. Remember, however, supplements are no replacement for a healthy diet.

Practicing Moderation

An individual's background and lifestyle often determine what he or she considers an acceptable use of a specific substance. For example, the use of alcohol is considered by many to be a natural part of social life. Used in moderation, alcoholic beverages can even have health benefits. But they may also be used, often to excess, to deal with stress.

Others look to prescription drugs to ease symptoms of stress or loneliness. When unable to obtain prescription drugs, they often resort to over-the-counter drugs in search of relief, but end up creating further health problems. Smoking is extremely detrimental to health, and yet one of the most difficult addictions to break.

Drug and alcohol abuse can, and often do, damage and even wreck lives. If you are reliant on a drug or alcohol, discuss your addiction with your doctor. Cut back, and keep trying to quit. If you need support, get it. The attractions of such harmful habits fade rapidly as you age, but the damage grows. This can make quitting easier. Try your best to conserve your money, energy, and health for other, better things.

Seeing Your Doctor

Stay up-to-date with medical checkups, including those for vision and hearing. Your doctor should advise you of key tests you should have at regular intervals. Be sure to have these tests done; inconvenient as they may seem at the time, they can save you from much worse. Become knowledgeable about medical issues related to aging. Be aware of signs that may warn of disease, and bring any symptoms you experience to the attention of your doctor immediately. Also be aware of the warning signs of mental health problems, such as depression or anxiety. If necessary, your doctor can refer you to a specialist.

Managing Stress

In many ways, life becomes less stressful with age. Experience brings ease to many challenges and situations that might have fazed you in your youth. Nevertheless, watch your stress levels. Chronic stress can lead to serious medical problems. The keys to keeping stress under control are maintaining a good diet, exercising regularly, getting enough sleep, and managing your time well. Take at least 20 minutes a day for yourself, whether to relax with a book or hobby, or to spend time helping others. Keep things in perspective: perfectionism, anger, being critical of others, and competitiveness can all lead to stress. Meditation or yoga are effective ways to reduce stress.

One of the more stressful situations you may encounter is caregiving. Approaches to handling the stress of caregiving are given in chapters 8 and 9.

Staying Safe and Secure

A safe and secure environment is always important. When you were very young, your parents probably put childproof catches on cupboards and installed stair guards. There were rails on your crib and your playpen to keep you safe. When you're older, there are new concerns. First and foremost, avoid slips and falls. Chapter 4 includes strategies to keep your home safe as you age.

Do you drive? In today's society, a car is a symbol of independence, and it can be quite inconvenient to get to some places without one. However, declining eyesight, reflexes, and mobility can put you and others at risk if you continue driving when you're no longer able to do so safely. These problems usually develop gradually, and often drivers are not aware of them.

As you age, at regular intervals, ask a trusted friend or relative to give you an honest opinion on your driving abilities. If he or she thinks there may be a problem, listen. If it is no longer safe for you to drive, there are many fast and inexpensive alternatives: subways, buses, commuter trains, taxis, and lifts from family, friends, neighbors, or community volunteer drivers. Whenever possible, walk, don't drive. Walking improves fitness and reduces stress.

Using Your Mind

The assumption that your mind will inevitably deteriorate after the age of 65, and that you will become senile, is unfounded. Dementia is not specifically related to aging. Most people still have the same ability to think, but their response times are slower.

You've likely heard the expression "Use it, or lose it." Some studies suggest that activities such as reading, going to the theatre, listening to the radio, playing games such as cards and checkers, doing crossword or jigsaw puzzles, and visiting museums reduce the likelihood of cognitive decline in old age.

A major US research project known as the Nun Study, conducted at the Sisters of Notre Dame School, in Mankato, Minnesota, is tracking the lives of almost 700 elderly nuns. Autobiographical essays written by nuns in their 20s, before they took their vows, have been scrutinized. Many of them who've lived very long lives without mental deterioration in old age, expressed more complex thinking and more positive emotions in their autobiographies. They have also tended to keep more mentally active by reading, playing cards, and doing word games.

It is not yet known whether the early development of the brain determines an individual's general level of mental activity and, also, his or her likelihood of developing dementia, or whether a life long positive outlook is a key to longevity and may delay Alzheimer's disease.

Many do believe that using their minds has preventive power. Few would disagree that the more a person uses their intellect and talents, the better they will develop, and that the pursuit of learning is inherently rewarding at any age.

Companionship

One of the great pleasures of growing older can be the increasing depth of personal relationships. In your teens and 20s, the special friendships that will be cherished throughout your life are usually just beginning. By middle age, you have friends you've had for decades; friends who really know you, and your history, and to whom you can tell anything. You've done many of the same things your parents did—raised children, enjoyed achievements and coped with disappointments, faced your own aging—and, whether your parents are still living or not, you can appreciate them in new ways. You have the pleasure of seeing your children, nieces and nephews, or your friends' children maturing into adulthood. You have more time for family and friends. These relationships can also be a vital source of support when facing a difficult situation. Sometimes, however, aging can bring stress to family relationships. Improving communication and understanding with family members is discussed in chapter 5.

Both emotional and physical intimacy are important throughout life, and for those who've shared a warm, loving relationship with a spouse or partner, the loss experienced upon death can be heart-wrenching. Although finding the right companion becomes more difficult, today, intimate relationships—and weddings—are regular occurrences in retirement and nursing homes.

Eva, a 62-year-old spinster who sang in a church choir, met and married a recently widowed minister. She blossomed, radiating a glow that inspired those around her.

Carole, a widow, had been confined to a wheelchair for over 20 years. Having reviewed her situation carefully, she made an appointment with an orthopedic surgeon who told her that, if she were to have both knees replaced, there was a good chance she'd walk again. Carole took that chance and created a whole new life for herself. Fully recovered from the successful operation, she booked a Caribbean cruise where she met her future second husband.

Give your personal relationships the attention they deserve. Enjoy the new perspectives aging gives them. And continue to make new friendships, with people of all ages. When you were younger, did you have older friends who mentored you or expanded your view of life? Perhaps now it's your turn. Having a cache of younger friends adds spice and interest to life.

When Stefan was in his 30s, he befriended a man who was 20 years his senior. Today, at 58 and 81, they're still friends, and now Stefan is cultivating younger friends who enrich his life with their enthusiasm and joie de vivre.

Appearance

Does how you look affect how you feel? For most people, it does. It's natural to tend to deny the physical signs of aging: the wrinkled brow, drooping eyelids, sagging neck, thickening waistline, and widening hips. "It can't be happening to me," you say, but it is. Hollywood plastic surgeons do a fabulous job at reconstructing aging stars. Then there are those like Robert Redford, who says he's proud of his wrinkles and has no intention of changing the way he looks. Do you consider Tina Turner old? How about Goldie Hawn or Sean Connery? These celebrities offer a much more positive slant on aging. Many find one of the real benefits of growing older is that they no longer worry about their appearance so much. And that means more time and money for important things.

If you feel negative about aging, look around you. The average 65-year-old today looks younger than a 50-year-old did a generation ago. Who says older people are unattractive and unsexy? Maybe aging isn't so bad after all.

Learning, Working, Sharing

A common myth about aging is that seniors don't contribute much to society. Those who are retired continue to contribute to society in a myriad ways—as voters and taxpayers, consumers, parents and grandparents, consultants and corporate directors, artists, audiences and patrons, volunteers, and in a multitude of other ways. Some simply don't believe in retirement. They plan to keep working all their lives, either because they love their work and want to stay productive, or because they need or want the money, or a combination of the two. More and more seniors are returning to the workforce after retirement; others, in ever-greater numbers, are just not stopping work when they hit 65. The advent of flex-time, job sharing, and working from home has dramatically increased options for continuing to work as you age. It may be that, not too far in the future, retirement will become a completely outmoded concept.

There are innumerable ways to stay involved and engaged in the world as you age. Today, individuals in their 70s and 80s are attending colleges and universities to earn undergraduate or graduate degrees. Some take courses with the aim of acquiring a degree, others to follow a personal interest or develop a talent or skill. Increased leisure time is one of the great rewards of retirement. Finally, there's more time to spend with family and friends, pursue interests, and enjoy the things you worked hard for. You may have more money to spend on yourself than before, particularly if you've planned ahead or decide to keep working part-time. Increasingly, there are magazines, radio and television shows, and Internet Web sites geared toward the 50+ population, featuring content on innumerable topics related to aging, including lifestyles, medical concerns, food, and health. For those who belong to the American Association of Retired People (AARP), there are discounts for insurance, travel, and other major purchases.

> Mariko bought her first computer as a present to herself when she turned 81 and enjoys e-mailing her contacts worldwide. When she's not on her computer, she's off on Elder Hostel vacations, taking courses, and meeting new friends. She's always attuned to the activities available in her city and takes full advantage of many events each month.

In your working years, it's important to set aside leisure time to pursue interests that can engage you throughout your life. Most people, when asked to describe themselves, begin by saying what they do, their career or position in life. When that's removed by job loss or retirement, some people feel a loss of identity, or no longer needed.

> Although Charles, a CEO at a large insurance company, had organized many retirement-planning programs for his employees, he hadn't made time to attend to his own needs. Upon retirement, he found himself devastated because his talents were no longer required. He had the

insight to seek professional help, do some serious self-examination, and develop new interests.

Do you fear facing empty hours each day? Do you think you're too old to learn new things and change? There's no need to sit alone listening to the clock tick. What have you dreamed of doing, but were unable to in the past because of work and career obligations? Do it now. Find out about continuing education options available in your community or online that might interest you; the variety of choices is amazing. Launch a second career or turn a hobby into a business.

Gabrielle took up stained glass as a hobby in her 50s. Today, in her late 60s, she receives commissions for her work.

Victor retired from teaching shop at a vocational school to become a superb cabinetmaker. At 75, he says, "I used to work five day weeks, now I work seven."

On the other hand, never be busy just for the sake of it. Try to save some time each day for reflection, exploring your inner self, and appreciating and savoring the world around you.

If you're having difficulty focusing on a plan of action, consider working with a personal coach. Personal coaches help individuals deal with everything from career and retirement adjustment to business building and personal effectiveness. To find a personal coach, go to www.coachfederation.org, where a personal coach can be found anywhere in the world, to assist with any number of situations. Before choosing a personal coach, make certain that coach is accredited with this federation.

Volunteering, essential to the survival of many important organizations in almost every sector, can add tremendous dimension to life. Today, corporations are becoming more and more committed to encouraging employees to take on volunteer roles. These can be extended into retirement. Find a worthy cause or charity where your time and abilities can make a difference.

Beth worked at a bank and once a week volunteered to deliver Meals on Wheels. When she retired, she continued to do this, not only because it helped the recipients of the meals—for some shut-ins, she was the only link to the outside—but also because it boosted her own self-esteem.

Each individual is part of their place and time, and has an impact on it. Make yours a positive one. Speak out when you feel strongly about an issue. Write letters expressing your views. Get involved in local or national groups working for change in areas that interest or concern you. In your own life, model the type of world you'd like to see.

Volunteering, community involvement, political activism, participation in a religious community, membership in clubs, and continuing education are all excellent ways to stay involved in life and meet new people—some like you and others different from you, of all ages—at all stages of life.

4

Where Will You Hang Your Hat?

Your lifestyle is, to a large degree, determined by where you live, and any move to a new location can be very stressful, regardless of your age. The older you get, the more daunting it can become. Physical surroundings have a strong effect on your feeling of well-being, self-esteem, and sense of identity. This is why so many seniors cling to the notion of remaining at home as long as possible, even when it may no longer be to their advantage. Many seniors' communities are springing up in urban and rural areas, making more choices available to seniors. In the coming years, as baby boomers become elder-boomers, the housing options for seniors are expected to increase dramatically. Boomers tend to have much higher expectations than do those of earlier generations, and they're used to having their demands met. They will not accept less than the best. That means the marketplace will have to change to accommodate their needs and desires.

Making the Right Choice

Making the right choice is always a concern, at any stage of life. Decisions about a home represent a major commitment and must be given the utmost consideration. Everyone cherishes his or her independence and, whether young or old, hopes to maintain it as long as possible. Seniors often think, "I know I should move to a smaller place, but where?"

> "When Ivan and I married," says Agnes, a 74-year-old widow, "we purchased a small bungalow that was quickly replaced by a larger home when our family outgrew it. As Ivan moved up the ladder in his company, we moved to a yet larger home. Now I'm alone and must start the process downward to a more suitable place."

Elements of your physical environment that affect your quality of life—the region in which you live, the type of housing you choose, and whether you live in an urban or rural location—can influence your aging process. Environment is determined to a considerable degree by income, which affects people's choice of housing, mode of transportation, and socialization. Your attitudes and values will also play a large role in how you decide to meet your changing needs.

What means the most to you? If you own a house, is it the garden you'd miss? The memories? The neighborhood? Having everything the way you like it? Do you feel overwhelmed by what moving will entail? Do you have pets? Or social activities you want to stay close to? Can you drive, or do you need to be close to public transportation? Do you have disabilities that will have an impact on your decision? Where will you feel most safe and secure? Reflect on your priorities and make a list of what you like and dislike about your current residential situation. Could there be another situation that could give you more of what you want and less of what you don't want?

Who else will your decision affect, and does it matter? How important is it to you to be near family or friends? With today's busy lives, an extra couple of hours travel time can be difficult for many people to find. If you have a daughter, say, who would like to see you regularly and whom you would like to see, and she doesn't drive, think about this before you move further away. Don't underestimate the difference this can make to how often, and for how long, friends and relatives may be able to visit.

If you're thinking of moving to a new city, don't forget that this will mean finding a new doctor, hairdresser, optician, and chiropractor, a new market, church, swimming pool, club, or favorite bookshop and café. Even a move to another part of town will require many such changes, and it can be challenging to find satisfactory replacements.

> "I would dearly love to live closer to my son and his family, but to move there would be very expensive," says Isabel, a 75-year-old who was recently widowed.

Moving to be nearer to family is not always the right choice. Long-time friends, a familiar neighborhood, and closeness to necessary services cannot be easily replaced.

If going to the theatre, opera, symphony, ballet, movies, art galleries, museums, and other cultural events is central to your life, it's important to consider their proximity.

Many seniors considering relocation rate closeness to higher education as a major factor. Life-long learning opens doors to the world: new people, new ideas, and new interests.

When relocating, many seniors also consider proximity to a cardiac unit, not just nearness to a hospital or medical center. Cardiac conditions are common among seniors. Should you decide to relocate, make certain there is adequate medical attention available should you require it.

During his working years, Paul, a business manager of a large telephone company, spent endless weekends winterizing his cottage in a remote northern area, preparing for his retirement. The cottage was located on a beautiful lake, surrounded by a wonderful forest for hiking all year round. Paul's retirement date fell in late spring; he sold his house in the city in time to move north at the beginning of the summer. He and his wife, Susan, were happy to be away from the hustle and bustle of the city and invited many friends to visit and stay with them. But when the summer cottage crowd went back to the city in the fall, the couple had no neighbors or contacts nearby. They were lonely. The cottage was not close to stores or other conveniences. Then, just before Christmas, Paul had a massive stroke. Although Susan contacted the local ambulance, the small community hospital was not equipped to handle Paul's case, so he had to be airlifted to a medical center. Today, he's being cared for by Susan in a rented apartment in the city. Sometimes, they're able to go up to the cottage when their adult children can assist them, but that doesn't happen very often.

Find out ahead of time what your preferred options cost so you can save appropriately. Costs can vary widely. What will be covered? What else will you need to budget for? Be aware that costs may increase significantly; you don't want to find yourself someday unable to pay for dental care, haircuts, or gifts for your grandchildren. If family members will be assisting you, be sure to talk frankly about financial strategies and limitations.

Often the reason a family home is sold is to provide capital for the "golden years." The sale will determine the amount of available funds and what can be afforded in a new location. Will those proceeds be used to purchase a smaller home, a condominium, or used as investment income? Should the money be invested with the help of a financial advisor to enable you to continue to live in the manner you have grown accustomed to? Would renting out the family home and moving into a smaller abode be a more appropriate route to financial freedom? Again, a financial advisor can help you make the right decision.

These are just some of the questions that will need to be addressed before you make any decision regarding your future housing needs.

Staying in Your Own Home

Ideally, most people want to live out their lives at home, in the house or apartment where they know the neighbors, are familiar with local businesses and organizations, and like where they live; a neighborhood, where people of all ages live together in a sort of harmony.

Remaining Independent

Many strategies and services can extend your independent time in your own home, often right to the end of your life. You can have groceries, prescription drugs, dry cleaning, and many other things delivered; send out laundry, particularly big projects like washing pillows and duvets; use taxis and car services; and hiring a maid service to clean the kitchen, bathroom and vacuuming. All of this could transform your life. Electronic tools such as cell phones and microwave ovens could also help you retain your independence.

If you don't have Internet access, consider getting it. You can now shop for almost anything and do most financial transactions online. A wealth of entertainment options and online clubs, for example, online bridge tournaments can also be accessed. The Web is also a great source of up-to-date information on health and aging. Many institutions now offer online continuing education. If you can't afford the up-front costs of a computer, modem, and Internet software, consider a lease-to-buy arrangement, to spread the costs over time. If you don't know how to use a computer or surf the Web, take a course. Many are free and there are courses designed especially for senior novices. Find one at your local library, school, community center, or through advertisements.

Adapting Your House

Rearranging and renovating your home can extend your independence. Have a washroom installed on the ground floor; at the same time, bring your laundry facilities up from the basement. Hire someone to do yard work and line up a handyman. Reorganize your shelves and cupboards to ensure you have enough easy-to-reach storage space. Are your fridge and freezer big enough to allow you to cut down on the number of trips to the grocery store? There are many ways to make household chores less onerous and strenuous, at any age.

If you plan to stay in your own house or apartment, make sure it's safe and secure.

• Improve the lighting at outdoor entrances, and make sure the locks work easily.

• Install handrails on stairs, both inside and out, on both sides of the staircase. Make certain the height is comfortable for you. Remember, people's height tends to decrease with age. There should be a light switch at both the top and bottom of any stairs.

• Remove scatter rugs, stair runners, and mats, or ensure they are secure, not free to move about. Purchase shoes and slippers with non-skid soles.

• Many accidents occur in the bathroom. Install a hand-held shower that's easy to reach. Put grab bars at the side of the bathtub on a 45° angle and at the end for easy in and out access. As you age, keeping your balance may become more difficult. If lowering yourself to sit in the bathtub creates a problem, use a tub seat. A non-slip mat in the tub will also increase safety. For balance and mobility issues, a raised toilet seat and grab bars beside the toilet are good ideas. Most of these items can be purchased through a medical supply house, which can be located through the Yellow Pages.

• The kitchen, a place where much time is spent, must be easily negotiable. Make certain food preparation areas are well lit. Perhaps the kitchen counters could be lowered, with an area to accommodate a chair to enable you to sit down while preparing food. Avoid using cupboards that require a step-stool. Install smoke and carbon monoxide detectors and make certain the batteries are working. Get a kitchen timer to remind you things are on the stove and use appliances with an automatic shut-off feature. Purchase a small kitchen-type fire-extinguisher and make certain you know how to use it.

• Personal alarm systems can be lifesavers if a fall occurs or a situation arises that you can't manage. They can be purchased outright or rented.

• Check all electrical outlets and switches, light bulbs, space heaters, and wood-burning stoves to ensure they're in good working order. Keep all electrical and telephone cords away from where they could be tripped over.

• Make sure telephone areas are well lit and that emergency numbers are by each phone.

• Have a phone and a smoke detector on each floor of your house.

• Have an emergency exit plan that you can manage easily, and be sure to have somewhere you can go in an emergency.

Depending on its size and design, you could have your house converted into two or even three apartments, and use the ground-floor apartment for yourself. This could make particular sense if you plan to be away a lot; the house is occupied and there is someone to handle emergencies. The extra income could pay for the costs of renovation.

Some Factors for Homeowners to Consider

• Being a homeowner is essentially a lifestyle decision. There are many ways you can make your money grow besides owning real estate.

• You may have needed a large home when your children were young, but do you still?

• Perhaps you've paid off your mortgage, but the many costs to owning a house—upkeep, taxes, heating, utilities, insurance—can really add up.

• How long do you want to be digging up weeds, raking leaves, and shoveling snow—or paying someone else to do these chores? Will you be able to afford to pay someone to handle the upkeep when you can no longer do so? An apartment or condo with a balcony garden, located next to a beautiful park, could be just as satisfying, and far more manageable.

• Are shopping, cooking, cleaning, and doing housework tasks you enjoy? If not, moving to a retirement home might liberate time and energy for things you find more rewarding.

• Do you plan to travel a lot, or be away from home much? Who will look after your house while you're away?

• Do you want somewhere for your out-of-town family or friends to stay when they visit? How often will that be? Hotel costs during such visits might be much less than the costs of maintaining a house year round.

• Are you counting on people being there who may not be? A key factor in your decision to stay in your home may be wanting to remain near a favorite neighbor, but can you be sure your friend will never move away? Be realistic about other people's priorities.

• If your spouse or partner dies before you do, you may find yourself feeling very isolated living alone in your own home. Plan for this possibility.

• If you want to live in your own house, is the one you're in now the best one for your current and future needs? Perhaps a smaller home, a bungalow, would suit you better than your current three-story Victorian—if not now, in the near future.

Try to make your decisions sooner rather than later. Often, people wait far past the optimum time to move. You want to stay in control, and make decisions that increase your options and independence.

Buying a Condominium

Condominiums are chosen because they offer freedom from many of the worries of home maintenance. No more grass to cut or snow to shovel. No need to wonder if the roof needs replacing or the driveway resealing. Choosing one with 24-hour security is a good idea if you head south in the winter.

Some condominiums have extensive recreational facilities: a pool, tennis courts, a sauna, or golf course. They may have a clubhouse or recreation room where members and owners can play cards or rent space for parties or family gatherings.

Of course, these are all factored into the overall cost of the condominium. Bear in mind that condo fees are not fixed and are based on amenities within the complex. Decide before you buy what lifestyle suits you best.

Continuing Care Retirement Community (CCRC)

Continuing Care Retirement Communities are sometimes called life care communities. Entering one is usually a once-in-a-lifetime choice and that's the appeal. Many have large campuses that include separate housing for those who live very independently, assisted living facilities that offer more support, and nursing homes for those needing skilled nursing care. With all on the same grounds, people who are relatively active, as well as those who have serious physical and mental disabilities, all live nearby. Residents then move from one housing choice to another as their needs change.

While usually very expensive, many guarantee lifetime shelter and care with long-term contract that detail the housing and care obligations of the CCRC as well as its costs.

Renting an Apartment or Condominium

Renting may allow you to stay in the heart of the neighborhood you're part of. This can be a very good housing option for seniors who go south each winter. It also gives freedom from dealing with the general maintenance concerns of home-ownership; those are the responsibility of the building owner.

How satisfactory this option is will depend on how responsible and responsive your landlord is. Living in a private apartment in someone else's home, for example, can be ideal, or a nightmare; tenants can find themselves dealing with unwanted noise, smells, vermin, and problems with heating and repairs. Similarly, apartment buildings vary enormously in the level of service and security provided.

If you're a first-time renter, become familiar with the act governing landlord and tenant responsibilities in your municipality. Try to find your apartment through friends or an agent, rather than the newspaper. If possible, speak to the previous tenant to discover any problems he or she may have had.

Seniors' Communities

These are enclaves (gated and otherwise) that offer a mix of housing choices, such as bungalows, condominiums, and apartment living. Most offer a community center for activities and, often, a golf course. A downside of this type of housing is that, as you age, your health may deteriorate, necessitating a level of care not always available in this setting. Or, you many want to see younger people as well as older people around you; youth adds vitality to any community. However, for those who prefer no children in their lives, this is an ideal solution. Some developers recognize the need to provide a retirement home wherein care can be given without the client moving beyond their familiar surroundings. For couples, this can be ideal, as they aren't separated when the health of one deteriorates.

Retirement Homes

Retirement homes are intended for seniors who are still basically independent. They offer security, freedom from household chores, and a community. Many social activities and recreational programs provide a great way to become involved and socialize with peers. Retirement homes come in all shapes and sizes, and usually offer either semi-private or private accommodation. Newer homes often have larger units, or suites, with a sitting room as well as a bedroom. Retirement homes can be found in both urban and rural settings; the right location for you will depend on your lifestyle.

Today, retirement homes are recognizing that, as people age, they do become more frail, and that some residents may require additional care. Many are offering assisted-living programs within their facilities. Although no one likes to acknowledge that his or her faculties may decline, when considering a retirement home, look for one that provides at least some level of care.

Finding the Right Fit

When is the best time to move to a retirement home? Below are some of the things to consider.

• Can you afford the monthly cost of a retirement home? If it's outside your capability, are there subsidies available to you?

• What type of care is provided, should it be needed? Is there 24-hour nursing coverage? Do only qualified personnel give out medications? Is there a doctor responsible for the residents' care? Can residents retain their own physician?

• Are there recreational programs suitable for seniors? Is

there adequate staff to provide such programming?

• Does the facility provide special diets for diabetics or people with cardiac conditions? Is a dietician available to the staff?

• Is the facility equipped to cope with special needs?

• Does the retirement home belong to an organization that governs its operation? Is there is a professional regulating body? Does the facility meet the regulating-body's standards?

Before you make such a major change in lifestyle, consider arranging for a trial period of at least a week to find out if the facility suits you. This will give you an opportunity to meet the other residents and learn firsthand how well they enjoy living there.

Moving in with Family

In some cases, an elderly parent will expect to move in with an adult child, or an adult child will want his or her parent to move in. Sometimes, this transition is one of ease and is acceptable to all family members, who welcome the senior with open arms. In other families, this decision is made with more ambivalence, either on the part of the adult child or the parent. There is much potential for both happiness and unhappiness in such an arrangement, which is discussed in depth in chapter 5.

Long-Term Care Facilities

Lei, an 87-year-old, is suffering from a cognitive impairment, and has an only daughter, Shirley, who works full-time. Shirley lives in a small one-bedroom apartment. When it became evident Lei could no longer live alone in her house, Shirley researched facilities that offered a warm and caring environment, where some of Lei's friends had moved. The outcome proved successful for both of them. Lei is happy in her new home, and Shirley has peace of mind knowing her mother is well cared for.

Shirley visits twice a week and, sometimes on Sunday evenings, takes Lei home to her apartment for dinner. This suits them both, allowing them a quality of life they can both enjoy.

When you become physically frail and require assistance with bathing, grooming, dressing, and eating, or grow mentally frail and demonstrate signs of cognitive impairment, or if you're suffering from a serious medical condition such as cancer, stroke damage, chronic heart disease, or Alzheimer's disease, it may be time to look for a long-term care facility, or nursing home, that can serve your needs.

While this can be a difficult decision, it's unquestionably the best solution for many families. In these facilities, you can be with friends, have programs suitable to your changing needs, and family members can visit regularly.

All long-term care facilities must meet specific requirements concerning fire and safety, food preparation, and staffing. However, there are differences in the quality of nursing care provided, level of access to mental health and rehabilitative services, and ability to care for those with complex physical disabilities.

Visit the facilities in your neighborhood first. It's best to be in familiar territory if at all possible. Look at the condition of the home, talk to other residents, and ask a lot of questions. Try to obtain a copy of the most recent state survey of the facility to learn if it has been cited for deficiencies. Most likely, the preferred choice will have a long waiting list, meaning it could take upwards of two years to secure a bed in a long-term care facility. Be prepared to have a list of choices and recognize the first choice may not be available. Most important, plan ahead. For a free copy of the American Association of Retired Person's (AARP) "Solving Nursing Home Problems: A Guide for Families" (D17065), send a request to AARP Fulfillment, EE01522, 601 E St. NW, Washington, DC 20049. Include the publication title, stock number and your mailing address.

Planning the Move

Whether you're 18 and going off to college, or 80 and moving into a retirement home, and whether your destination is another country, a new city, or around the block, any move is extremely stressful. It will work out best, and the transition into your new home will be easiest, if it's a planned process.

> "I've lived in this house for 35 years. Your father and I moved here just after we were married, and you four children were all raised here. How can I give it up?" said Celia, an 85-year-old widow, as she discussed with her daughter how, ever since her husband died, she really couldn't manage her big house anymore. She had decided to move into a local retirement home, but was totally bewildered about where to start.

It's been said, "We spend the first half of our lives collecting our possessions and should spend the last half giving them away." Sage advice, but difficult to follow. If you've been avoiding making decisions about your belongings, it may be time to begin.

Often, heirlooms will not have the same meaning for your children as they have for you, nor may they have much other appeal. Today's lifestyles are much more casual, and the silver tea service you've treasured, or your beautiful, fancy china, although quite valuable to a collector, may not be as appealing to your son or daughter.

Find a reputable antique dealer (preferably through a recommended source) who can evaluate those items you no longer need or want. Once you've made the decision to part with certain items, ask family members if they want any of them. Adult children often like to choose a few items with personal meaning. The rest can be disposed of through other means.

Keep in mind that the evaluated value of an item can be

quite different from its appraised value for selling. For example, Great Aunt Julia's antique samovar may be evaluated at a rather substantial amount for insurance purposes, whereas, when it's sold, the appraised value will be much lower.

Hazel paid $40 to learn that her china tea set was worth $700. However, when she asked the appraiser what he would give her for it, he offered $300, so she decided to keep it in the family.

Never pay to store items. These items are easily forgotten and you'll end up with costly rental fees.

Decide what you want to take to the new location. Ensure all items are well packed, preferably by a professional mover, before being moved from your present location. Rushed packing can lead to damage. If you need help with packing (or unpacking) and can't afford to hire someone, ask relatives or friends. Most people are willing to contribute some help to this kind of big, one-time project. Be sure to obtain adequate packing materials before you begin.

When Elizabeth unpacked after moving across the country, she was crestfallen to find a unique stained-glass lamp shade had not been properly crated, resulting in irreparable damage. The lamp shade had been a wedding present.

Movers do have some insurance, but if the objects being moved are important to you, it's always wise to purchase more coverage. There may be a few fine pieces or particularly valuable items that you choose to ship separately, by a more secure method, or even carry with you to your new destination.

If you're moving into a smaller setting, you'll definitely need to make some firm decisions about what's truly needed as opposed to what you'd like to take. For example, you won't require cooking utensils in a retirement setting, but you may want to have a few cups and saucers on hand to entertain family and friends.

Items you no longer need, including furniture or appliances, which aren't appropriate for resale, could be donated to a favorite charity, which will bring you a tax deduction.

Make a list of everyone who needs to be notified of your move. At the top of your list, put canceling or changing utilities such as heat, electricity and cable. The telephone company also needs lead time to ensure you have continuous service. By notifying the post office, you can have mail redirected to your new address. Be sure to let your friends and other significant individuals such as doctor, lawyer, banker, dentist, and pharmacist know your new address. Write or have postcards cards printed and do one large mailing.

Frequently, the news media reports negative stories about aging—the insufficient number of nursing-home beds, or how many seniors are sick. Fewer than 10% of seniors live in long-term care facilities. That means most are still living independently. They access resources to suit their individual needs, and work together with family members to make the most of their options and opportunities.

5

The Ties That Bind

Aging is a process that affects the whole family. As your parents age—and as you, in turn, age—you'll face many situations and decisions in which, to achieve the best possible outcome, the input of all affected family members will be needed. To make good decisions, families need to plan ahead. Family members also need to be able to communicate well with one another. Each person has strong feelings and desires that need to be recognized if everyone is to be satisfied with the decisions made.

Parent–Child Relationships

You're about to go into a meeting at work, when your phone rings. It's your father saying, "My car won't start and I have to go to the dentist." You may immediately drop everything to go see what's wrong with the car, or you may say, "Take a taxi, and I'll drop by on my way home from work." If your father ruled the roost, as an adult child you may find it difficult to say no to him.

"If you love me, you'll take care of me," your mother might say. But what if you don't love her? What if you resent the way you were raised and don't like the kind of person your mother is? Some adult children rarely, if ever, visit their parents.

Parents may use guilt to manipulate a loving adult child. "Honey, I'd really like to go visit your Aunt Sadie." You don't particularly care for Aunt Sadie, but your mother did a lot for you when you were growing up and gave in to your many wishes, so, out of guilt, you take her to see Aunt Sadie.

Or, you may be responsible not only for yourself but for dependent adult children, or grandchildren, and filled with anxiety about how your dependents will cope when you're gone.

You may need help but not want or know how to ask for it. In families where keeping a stiff upper lip is expected, reluctance to admit problems, coupled with an inability to openly discuss concerns, can make for strained relationships. It may take a crisis to open the doors of communication even slightly.

There are no perfect families.

Communicating Across Generations

The communication styles of earlier generations often didn't allow for open expressions of anger, resentment, lust, or other messy feelings. Real meaning was often veiled in euphemisms—and "nice" people didn't air their laundry in public. Dad obeyed the boss, mom obeyed dad, and the kids obeyed everyone. Children were seen and not heard.

The baby boom brought social revolution: new ideas about individual rights, women's rights, then children's rights; new attitudes toward spending and saving, work and play; new manners and mores. Today, fathers, mothers, daughters, and sons alike expect to be respected and listened to, to speak their minds openly, and to have their needs and ideas valued, and each is expected to respect the rights and needs of the others.

An understanding—by both seniors and adult children—of these changing styles of communication can be helpful as you begin to discuss the issues that confront you.

Planning Together

The earlier you and your family discuss issues together, the more time you'll have to consider options and come up with the best plan. If necessary, make the first move. Don't wait until a crisis occurs. Get the family together to begin discussing the issues that affect all of you.

First, each family member concerned should:

• be as informed as possible about the issues and options being discussed;

• think about how he or she feels about the situation, and what's most important to him or her;

• think about how others in the family may feel about the situation.

Then, together as a family:

• discuss the issues, in person, by letter or e-mail, or by phone;

• come up with options. Look at the pros and cons of each. Be realistic about what's possible and likely (try to avoid pipe dreams). Don't expect to resolve everything at once;

• avoid talking about the plan for a week or so to let it simmer;

• work on the plan again, take a break, work on it, and so on, until everyone agrees;

• make sure everyone understands the final plan and his or her role in it. Write it out (point form is fine) and give everyone a copy;

• include a plan for contingencies;

• review the plan at regular intervals, perhaps once a year, and update it if necessary.

Communicating with Family Members

Be honest about what you want and need—first with yourself, then with your family.

Let everyone have their say. Listen not for what you want to hear but for what others may be trying to say. Sometimes, you may need to read between the lines. Recognize that many of these issues can be difficult to discuss and it may take time for some family members to be able to articulate their needs or feelings.

Respect others' needs and opinions. This can be very difficult when their opinions differ widely from yours or when there are competing needs. Try to see things from other points of view and keep an open mind. There may be reasons for another's feelings or views that you're not aware of. Ask that person to help you understand.

Try to face issues head-on, and encourage others to do so.

Factors That Can Impair Communication

• Fear: Often, family members fear that if they say what they really want, they'll be seen as uncaring, greedy, lazy, or financially inadequate.

• Privacy: Many people are very uncomfortable discussing their financial situations, or health with others. Inquiring about others' finances or health may be even more taboo.

• Modesty: Individuals who are reluctant to draw attention to themselves, or who've always put others' needs ahead of their own, may be hesitant to express their own needs.

• Shame: An individual may be embarrassed to admit that he or she needs help, or is unable to help, particularly financially.

• Disrespect: An individual may fail to recognize the right of others to be considered in the decisions that affect them, or their rights to independence and responsibility.

• Unresolved conflicts: A family member may be nursing a grudge about something that happened in the past, or be unhappy with a current situation. They may feel neglected, angry, taken advantage of, or mistreated, and not be ready to work cooperatively while this situation remains unresolved.

• Distrust: One family member may believe another will not be honest; they may think, rightly or wrongly, that the other has a hidden agenda.

• Dishonest: A family member may have a hidden agenda.

• Dissociation: Some family members may feel the situation is not their responsibility.

• Personality: Every family has members who are more assertive than others and who, knowingly or unknowingly, intimidate more diffident family members.

How can these problems be resolved? Discuss them as a family, emphasizing that the purpose of working together is to benefit everyone. Agree that no one will be judged for expressing him or herself honestly, that everyone's needs are important, and that old squabbles should be set aside, at least temporarily, in the interest of the task at hand.

If you're one of the stronger personalities in the family, be aware of how your confidence, an asset in so many situations, might be intimidating, and take special care not to dominate the agenda. Although people who take a long time to form opinions and come to decisions can be irritating to more forceful, decisive individuals, for the same reasons, their ideas can be valuable and have nuances that might be missed if they're not given the time and encouragement to express their thoughts.

Agree at the outset that if anyone proves unable to bring constructive attitudes to your meetings, you'll have no alternative but to continue the process without them.

Meet together regularly as a family to determine one another's needs and develop a plan to follow in the event of a crisis. If you run into serious difficulties, consider inviting a mediator with experience in the issues you're debating, to buffer the situation, help open communication, and get everyone's needs and wants out on the table for discussion. Many different kinds of professionals—lawyers, doctors, psychologists, financial advisors, social workers, clergy, geriatric care managers, or other senior care consultants—have mediation training and experience. Try to find someone with whom everyone feels comfortable.

Family conflicts can arise over many issues. Common causes of unhappiness include the sale of the family home, bequests and legacies, second marriages and new relationships, the financial dependence of a family member or other financial problems, a senior coming to live with an adult child, and differences in attitudes and beliefs.

Selling the Family Home

What may be a liberating decision for you, may be a painful one for your children. The house they grew up in is likely filled with cherished memories. They might never have realized that it might not always be there for them to revisit. Unreasonable as it may seem, they may be angry when you announce your decision to sell your home.

If you find yourself in this situation, let your children know that the home is also filled with your precious memories of the life you shared with them. Sit down with your children and discuss your memories. Explain to them why this is the right change for you. Give your children a chance to take photos, if they wish, before packing up; invite them to choose a few items from the house that they value. If you have a large family, you may wish to have a family reunion or party before the house is sold. That way, cousins, aunts, and uncles—and friends and neighbors—can bring their memories to share too.

Bequests and Legacies

Fighting over an estate can tear families apart. The instructions you leave in your will are a private matter, but discussing the possibilities ahead of time with your potential heirs can help you make decisions to ensure the desired results.

You may have possessions that seem insignificant to you but which have immense personal meaning to one of your children. Or, there may be items of considerable value that a son or daughter has an eye on. Problems multiply when you have a second family. Your children or other relatives may feel reluctant to let you know their wishes, because of discomfort at discussing death, fear that they'll seem to care more about your possessions than about you, or worst of all, that they're in a hurry to see you depart. But knowing which items mean the most to your heirs whom may help you make what can be difficult decisions. If you think there may be unhappiness about a decision you plan to make—for example, you have one fine piece of jewellery and two daughters—talking it over and explaining your reasoning can help avoid inadvertently causing pain or anger. Take the initiative and bring the matter up yourself.

Through such discussions, you may also discover that there are items you could give away now, or more significant contributions you could make. You may discover goals your children, grandchildren, or other loved ones have that you'd like to enable. Without discussion, this information might never be revealed. For example, you may have been planning to stay in your family home for the remainder of your life, because you want to leave it to an adult child. But living in the family home again may not be part of your child's plans. If so, he or she will likely sell the house upon your death, in which case, perhaps it was not the best decision for you to hold onto it. Had you sold your house at an earlier point, you might have been able to put a grandchild through university, help an adult child buy a bigger home for a growing family, or start a long-dreamed of business.

Now you're gone, but so are those opportunities. Doubtless your bequests and legacies will not go to waste, but could you have distributed your assets more effectively earlier? Often, there's no good reason why those you love should not benefit from your wise financial management before you die. Consider the possibilities and discuss them with your children.

For further information on estate planning, see chapters 6, 16, and Appendix B.

Second Marriages and New Relationships

Second marriages can be much happier than first marriages. Often, partners have greater self-knowledge than when they were younger and know better the kind of person who will best suit them and most love and value them for who they are. But unless care is taken, second marriages can also damage or even destroy existing family relationships. When money comes into the equation, the situation can become quite ugly. Major problems can arise when one or both partners have children from a previous marriage and the adult children grow concerned about the possible loss of their inheritance. Today, a prenuptial agreement is not uncommon. A prenuptial agreement is simple to execute and protects the interests of all parties (see chapter 6).

Geoff, a retiree with two adult children, was widowed in his early 70s. He spent winters in Arizona to get away from the cold. While in Arizona, he met Kate, another snowbird, with whom he began a relationship. By the time they returned to their northern home, Geoff had proposed to Kate and marriage plans were underway. Kate, a widow, had no children. Geoff's two adult children were happy that he'd found someone new.

Shortly after their marriage, Geoff and Kate each wrote a new will. Recognizing that a large part of his estate had been earned by his deceased wife, a home-maker and the mother of his children, Geoff took care of his adult children.

Within a few months, Geoff suffered a massive stroke. He was unable to speak and confined to a wheel-chair. Geoff's children, who were quite devoted to him, were regular visitors. They began to notice a change in Kate's response to them. She became much cooler, often suggesting they not visit because, "Geoff is too sick for company." They tried to appreciate that caregiving was difficult and wanted to honor Kate's wishes, but they still wanted to see their father.

Soon, Geoff died. At the reading of the will, Geoff's children were shocked to learn that Geoff had left every-thing to Kate. Unbeknownst to them, Kate had had Geoff change his will after he'd had the stroke. Kate got Geoff's entire estate, except for a few trinkets left to his adult children.

Many seniors embark on new relationships, including sexual relationships, late in life. Adult children are often uncomfortable thinking of their parents' sexuality. They may even think it unseemly for an older person to want sex. While sexual activity does tend to decline with age, there are tremendous individual differences. Chronological age isn't the critical factor in sexual activity or physical intimacy. Neither age, nor illness, nor demen-tia necessarily diminishes or extinguishes sexual desire. It's a normal and healthy part of being human, at all stages of life.

In her nursing home, Helga shared a room with Marie. Marie and Robert, also residents at that home, spent much time together. Helga recognized the importance of giving them privacy, so she'd always go to the library or solarium whenever Robert came to visit Marie. When

Helga's health improved enough to enable her to move into her own apartment, she told the staff that they should let Robert move into her old bed, so he and Marie could be together.

Financial Problems

Who will, and who should, help out when a family member is in financial difficulty? In some families, the answer will be everyone. In others, it may fall to the one best able to help, but it could also be simply the one most willing. Open communication and honest, informed, realistic strategizing are needed to arrive at a satisfactory decision. The best plan is for families to plan ahead, together, for this possibility. This will minimize the hardship and stress for all concerned.

If you're called on to help a family member, understand how humiliating it can be to need to ask for financial support. Try to communicate the happiness you feel at being in a position to help, even as you make sure to keep a balance between your own and your family member's needs.

If you need financial support from your family, be honest about what you need, and try to give as much advance notice as possible of the need. Don't underestimate the unspoken sacrifices that may be made on your behalf. Consider whether there are non-financial ways you might be able to offer something in return.

Living with Adult Children

Twice a week, Paulo and Francesca go to a local pub—an old haunt of Paulo's. Francesca is Paulo's adult daughter. Last year, after Francesca's mother died, her father went into a deep depression, neglecting his hygiene and nutritional needs, so Francesca asked her family doctor what to do. "Well," said the doctor, "you need to ask your father what he'd like." After much deliberation, Paulo agreed to move in with Francesca, her husband, and two teenage daughters. This wasn't easy on any of them, but as time passes, they're all adjusting to the new situation.

One of the options often considered by families when a parent no longer wishes to live alone, is to have them move in with an adult child. This is a decision that needs to be clearly thought through on the parts of both the parent and the adult child.

If the adult child lives in a two-story house, can the parent manage the stairs up to the bathroom several times a day, or will it be necessary to add a two-piece washroom on the main floor? Will it be necessary to install a stair-glide if the parent is, or becomes, unable to manage stairs?

Have you thought about the need for recreation and stimulation? Without peers, isolation can lead to depression. Visit local adult day-centres or seniors' recreation centres to see what programs are available.

What types of transportation exist in the community to get the parent to and from programs, shopping, and doctor's appointments? Allowing a parent to remain independent is the best thing an adult child can do. Adult children should involve their parents in decision making, letting them decide what they want to do, and trying to work out a schedule that respects everyone's needs. That means the parent must also compromise in some areas so that everyone's wishes and desires are accommodated. Co-operation is paramount.

Finances should be discussed in advance. Is the parent expected to help with expenses? If so, to what extent? Who determines the amount? Is it acceptable to both parties? Money, whether ample or insufficient, can be a bone of contention.

Living harmoniously can be difficult at the best of times when it entails parents and children. When a parent joins the household, new rules must be established. Privacy is a big issue. Children of all ages need space of their own, and when a grandparent moves in, it could mean doubling up with a sibling. If the siblings don't get along, there'll be additional problems. The parent also requires privacy, a place to go to rest during the day, to watch favourite TV programs, or just talk on the phone with friends. The adult child and his or her spouse, often both at work during the day, also need private space to relax. Finding adequate space for everyone means being resourceful and innovative.

The best results ensue when everyone has input into the new situation and how they feel their needs are, or are not, being met. What's expected of them in this new relationship? Often grandparents become a buffer zone between parents and children. Just as often, conflict arises over child-rearing beliefs and practices.

In recent decades, there've been tremendous advances in knowledge about how children grow and develop, that have led to major changes in child-rearing strategies. Evolving concepts of human rights have led parents and children to view the family as a democratic, rather than a hierarchical, structure. Desirable qualities for a child to grow up to possess have changed. At the same time, many age-old principles remain good guides for behaviour.

Adult children need to understand the different context in which their parents raised them. Grandparents need to accept gracefully that it is the right and responsibility of their adult child, and his or her spouse or partner, to raise their children the way they think best.

Tensions can also rise when children's needs and wishes are not taken into consideration. Let them have some say in how things should be. It's their life too.

Meals may be a challenge. Now, low-fat, low-salt, and low-cholesterol meals are required; these don't appeal to everyone's taste. Children need different foods to help them grow into healthy adults, and their needs must also be taken into consideration. The cook has to become very creative in meal planning.

These are just some of the issues that need to be put on the table before having a parent move in with an adult child.

Communication must be open and honest. Without open communication, everything else will break down, making the situation difficult to handle. There are social workers and gerontology specialists who offer counselling to help families adapt. It could take several sessions before true communication between adult children and their parents begins. Be patient. It's a new experience for everyone.

Taking a parent into an existing family environment can be both troubling and rewarding. It all depends on how each of you handles the transition. At worst, you'll bite your lip and endure the situation; at best, you'll learn to love and accept one another more fully. Hopefully, it will be the latter.

Differences in Attitudes and Beliefs

To work successfully together, family members must respect one another as individuals and grant one another the same fundamental rights.

You may feel a relative should be happy at your willingness to pay for a retirement home, and not appreciate how much independence means to them. Remember what your own independence means to you.

You may feel that the family is of paramount value, but others may value it less. You may feel that your parents should be giving more priority to you or your children in their plans, or that your adult children expect more from you than they should. For instance, you could be offended that a parent plans to move away from grandchildren, or an adult child from an older parent, and worry that you'll become distant. Everyone is different, and you can only decide what you want your own values to be. Don't forget, there are many ways for people to stay in touch and for families to build traditions. It may be time to find and build new, different ones.

Each person has many habits, good and bad. Often, individuals are unaware of their habits. If a family member's irritating habit is not destructive, try not to worry about it. If it's harmful, like smoking, encourage the individual to quit, certainly, but recognize that no one can live another person's life for them. In such a situation, it's quite acceptable to insist that there be no smoking in your presence, but otherwise, how you live your life is your responsibility, and how others live theirs is their own.

You may have a deep faith that you long to share with a loved one. Or, you may have no such belief, and find a relative's attempts to share their faith annoying. Faith is very personal. Respect and tolerate that of others, and, conversely, resist the impulse to proselytize. As much as possible, let each person approach their life in the way that he or she chooses. Difficult as this can be at times, live your life as you see right, and let others—including those you love—do the same.

6

Putting Your
Legal House
in Order

Who will make decisions for you when you no longer can? And how can you ensure that the decisions made are those you'd have made for yourself had you been able? How would you like your property and assets distributed after you die? How can you ensure that your wishes are honored? And who will be responsible for this?

This chapter presents legal issues relevant to aging. Your lawyer will look after these issues primarily; he or she may also work with your accountant, financial advisor and, perhaps, other professionals, such as your doctor, to ensure that your specific needs are met.

Role of Professionals

In the best of situations, your accountant will have your financial records and taxes and will be working with your financial advisor on your investments and financial planning. Your lawyer will act on your instructions; using knowledge obtained from your accountant and financial advisor, he or she will provide you with the legal options and documents to properly organize your present and future estate. If there are questions regarding your mental or physical capacity to instruct your advisors or make decisions, your physician may be called upon. Working as a team, you and these professionals can make the best possible arrangements for you, your loved ones, and your estate.

In dealing with professionals, remember that you, as the client, are in charge. You're entitled to be heard and make your decisions as you wish. Be wary of allowing a situation to arise in which a professional or relative starts making decisions for you. So long as you are mentally competent, you are entitled to make whatever decisions you feel like, no matter how odd they may seem to others, so long as you meet your legal obligations. If you're reading this book to learn about issues that affect a senior relative or friend, keep this advice in mind. Allow your parent, relative or friend to make their own decisions, as long as they are mentally capable. Remember that you'll be in the same position some day.

Power of Attorney

A will speaks for you from the grave; a Power of Attorney speaks for you while you're alive. A Power of Attorney is the vehicle that gives authority to another person to direct your affairs within the scope of the authority granted. Among other things, it may allow you to set in place controls that will carry on if you lose the mental capacity to fend for yourself and ensure that your interests are protected. In essence, a Power of Attorney is a document by which one person appoints a person to act on their behalf. The person who is appointed to act on behalf of another individual is called the "agent," and the person who appointed the agent is called the "principal."

Types of Powers of Attorney

There are four types of Powers of Attorney. The type you choose will depend on how much authority you want your agent to have; when you want your agent to start acting on your behalf; and when you want your agent's authority to come to an end.

• Limited Power of Attorney. Through a limited Power of Attorney you authorize another person to do specific things for you for a limited period of time, or in certain circumstances. The limited Power of Attorney ends if you become incapacitated or die. It also could end at a time that you specify in the document.
• General Power of Attorney. A general Power of Attorney gives another person the authority to do whatever you can do. Think very carefully before signing this type of document. This document ends when you become incapacitated or die.
• Durable Power of Attorney. A durable Power of Attorney authorizes your agent to continue to act for you after you become incapacitated. Ordinarily, a Power of Attorney is automatically revoked and the agent's power to act on behalf of the principal is terminated if the principal becomes incapacitated. However, a Power of Attorney may be made "durable" with proper wording. This means that the agent will continue to have the power to act despite the incapacitation of the principal.
• Springing Power of Attorney. A springing Power of

Attorney can be written so it goes into effect if you become incapacitated. Be cautious to clearly define how another will determine that the "springing event" has occurred.

Financial and Medical Powers of Attorney

You may want separate Powers of Attorney for finances and
health care. Within each legal document, you specify the terms
your chosen agent must follow in carrying out your wishes.
A durable Financial Power of Attorney allows your agent to
carry out financial tasks for you when you cannot do so. This
can include paying your bills, managing your property, and
handling other money matters.

A durable Medical Power of Attorney lets your agent make
medical decision for you when you can't make these decisions.

Detailed legislation sets out the requirements for a valid
Power of Attorney, the duties and responsibilities of the
appointed agent, and miscellaneous other details, such as
means of revocation, etc. While there are forms available, either
free from the government or for purchase, the cost of having a
lawyer prepare the documents for you is minimal, particularly
when the consequences of an improperly drafted document are
considered.

If your estate is small and you're married, you may be
under the illusion that your spouse will be able to handle things
if you become mentally incapacitated. This is not so. A spousal
relationship will not substitute for a Power of Attorney. Certain
powers, such as transfer of property, do not automatically pass
to a spouse. Should you lose your mental capacity, without a
Power of Attorney, it may, for example, be necessary for a court
application to be made to enable your spouse, or someone else,
to handle your financial affairs.

Capacity Issues

Mental capacity has many aspects. It's possible for a person to be incapable in one area, yet quite able to make decisions in another. The ability to make health decisions may be intact, while the ability to make property decisions is diminished; decisions regarding residence may be within your capability, while day-to-day care is not. For example, you decide to remain at home, but, despite your vociferous objections, you require regular visits by a home-care worker to ensure you eat correctly.

A properly drafted Power of Attorney can allow for these variations. The assistance of a lawyer, who'll listen to your wishes, can ensure self-sufficiency in those areas where capacity remains intact.

Capacity to Make a Power of Attorney

As in making a will, a person must have the mental capacity to make a Power of Attorney. In general, the following criteria should be met:

1. knowledge of the kind of property you have and its approximate value;

2. an awareness of obligations owed to your dependants;

3. knowledge that your agent will be able to do, on your behalf, anything in respect to property that you could do if capable, except make a will, subject to the conditions and restrictions set out in the Power of Attorney;

4. knowledge that the agent must account for his or her dealings with your property;

5. knowledge that, if capable, you may revoke the power.

Additionally, you should have the ability to understand whether the proposed agent has a genuine concern for your welfare and appreciates that you may need to have him or her make decisions on your behalf.

A lawyer taking instructions from a client has the obligation of ensuring that the instructions are given freely and are from a person who has the mental capacity to give those instructions. If there's any question regarding undue influence from a spouse or other interested party, it's prudent for the instructions to be given in a private interview between the lawyer and the client.

If there's any question regarding competency, it's best to obtain a formal assessment of mental capacity. There are trained, qualified individuals who can carry out this task. If capacity is shown, the assessment document will be useful should any future question arise regarding the validity of the Power of Attorney.

When Can the Power of Attorney Be Used?

The wording of a Power of Attorney will determine when it can be used. In general, a Power of Attorney without restrictions, can be used at any time. It is, therefore, of utmost importance that it be handled with appropriate care; preferably, it will be stored with a lawyer until needed. You should also keep a copy in your personal records.

The jurisdiction for laws concerning Powers of Attorney is by state; the detailed requirements can vary from state to state (your lawyer will advise you of the law in your state).

Choosing Your Agent

As your agent will be looking after all your financial affairs should you become mentally incapacitated, you will want to choose someone who is adept at handling financial matters. This agent should also be someone who understands your wishes.

If you have a spouse or partner, in most cases, this will be the person you choose; generally, he or she will understand both your financial affairs and your wishes. And, as your property matters are no doubt heavily entwined with those of your spouse, this would seem to be the most sensible choice for you both. If your financial affairs are complicated, you may consider appointing a professional, such as an accountant, lawyer, or trust company, as co-attorney with your spouse.

Others will likely choose a relative or close friend who meets the above criteria. Whomever you choose, it's prudent to also choose an alternate agent who can act if your original choice is unable. The same criteria as above should be met in choosing the substitute.

You may also consider appointing multiple agents. If you appoint two or more agents, you must decide whether the agents must act in concert in making a decision involving your affairs, or whether each may act independently.

Your agent should also be someone whom you're confident would make the same decisions for your care as you would have made for yourself. Here again, properly drafted documents can assist in setting out your wishes for your care.

You may decide to give your agent a general power for your care, or you may set out specific instructions, including what's referred to in some states as a "living will" and in others as "advance directives." These documents provide your directions for carrying out your wishes concerning medical intervention if you're terminally ill.

Restrictions

Your lawyer will be able to advise you about restrictions in your state regarding who may be an agent. Every state will provide for age, and there may be other qualifications. For example, someone who receives remuneration for the care of an individual shouldn't be appointed agent to look after that person's property.

Durable Powers of Attorney deal with situations in which you no longer have the mental capacity to make decisions affecting your property and/or care. Your appointed agent will look after these decisions and will be required to do so with the utmost care and with your best interests at heart.

It may be that you wish to place restrictions on those powers, or define the manner in which decisions are made, and you can do so. It's recommended that you do so with the assistance of your lawyer, who can ensure that the restrictions and your directions have the effect you wish.

Living Wills or Directives

As mentioned above, in addition to giving a Power of Attorney for Medical Care, you may provide a specific directive to ensure that you receive the medical care that you wish if you're terminally ill. An example would be a directive such as "Do not resuscitate" in certain cases. You may wish to have every possible treatment to keep you alive at any cost, or you may decide to be given only palliative care at a certain point in your terminal illness. A conversation with your doctor could provide you with the information you need. Your lawyer or doctor may assist you with this directive.

Having such a directive in place can remove the burden of responsibility from your loved ones, relieving them of difficult decisions at a time when they'll already be under a great deal of emotional stress.

Consent to Treatment

Consent to treatment is an area rife with complications for the medical profession. Obtaining proper consent in emergency situations can be a nightmare. Most states provide legislation to assist. At the top of this hierarchy is a guardian or person appointed under legislation, followed by an agent for personal care, then a board-appointed representative (if there's one) then a spouse or partner, then a child, then a parent, then a brother or sister, then any other relative. If none of these individuals are able or willing to give consent, the decision falls to the Public Guardian and Trustee. Given this hierarchy, it's most prudent, while you have the capacity, to appoint an agent who understands you and is likely to make the decisions you would have made.

Adult Guardianship

Where there is no Power of Attorney in place and an individual loses the capacity to make decisions either over property or personal care, it may be necessary to seek the court's assistance in appointing a guardian. This procedure is costly and time consuming. The result may be the appointment of a guardian who isn't the one you would have chosen to look after your property or care. In certain instances, where no suitable person has come forward to accept the role, the power may fall to the Public Guardian and Trustee.

Compensation

In most cases, an agent will be entitled to compensation, unless the document appointing your agent provides that there shall be none. As situations vary, your lawyer can provide you with the general guidelines regarding compensation that would likely apply to your estate. If compensation is accepted, your attorney will be held to a higher standard of care in carrying out his or her responsibilities, especially in making investments.

Wills and Trusts

While it's possible to make a valid will with a stationer's form, many things can go wrong. The serious consequences of having an invalid will, even in a "small" estate, far outweigh the cost of having a properly drafted will, prepared by a professional.

Mental Capacity

Among the requirements for making a valid will, are the formal ones; that it be in writing, that the person making the will be of legal age, that it is executed and witnessed. In addition to these requirements, there is the requirement of mental capacity. The determination of whether a person has the mental capacity to make a will is much the same as that for making a Power of Attorney. For example, knowledge of the kind of property he or she has, its approximate value, and an awareness of obligations owed to his or her dependants, as well as the ability to communicate instructions about what he or she wishes in the will, are all important considerations.

Not only must the person making the will (the "testator") have the mental capacity to give instructions, he or she must also be free to make those instructions without being influenced or coerced. It's the lawyer's duty, to the best of his or her ability, to make such an assessment before completing the will. If there's any question that the testator lacked capacity, or was coerced or unduly influenced, the will can be contested in court and may be found invalid. In such a case, the estate of the deceased will be dealt with under legislation, such as Guardianship or Conservatorship laws, and divided accordingly.

Selecting an Executor: Factors to Consider

Being an executor of a will can be an onerous job, requiring even-handed treatment of beneficiaries and an ability to deal with accounts and finances, as well as forms and documents. Look for an executor who's familiar with your property and one who knows you well enough to carry out your instructions as you would've wished. As with the selection of your agent in case of mental incapacity, it's likely that your first choice will be your spouse or partner, or a close friend or relative. Keep in mind that the person you choose will be required to take on the responsibility of dealing with all your property, both assets and liabilities. If you have a complex estate, you may wish to consider a professional, such as an accountant, lawyer, or trust company. Or, you may choose to have co-executors, one being your spouse, relative or personal friend, and the other a professional.

Your executor must be of the age of majority (this varies by state). It's best to choose someone residing in the state where your assets are located, to avoid requirements such as posting security with the court while the estate is being administered. You should also consider the possibility that your chosen executor may predecease you, become incapacitated, refuse, or otherwise be unable to take on the role. Provide the names of one or more alternate executors to be appointed to carry out the task.

Further considerations in choosing an executor include both the size and complexity of your estate. If there are assets such as business holdings, major investments, trusts, or other complexities, the use of a professional, with or without a co-executor, should be considered. An executor who is familiar with your wishes and the assets and liabilities of the estate, will be at an advantage and will be better able to carry out the provisions of your will as you intended.

Along with his or her authority, an executor must be able to handle serious responsibilities. Those responsibilities are governed not only by ethics, but also by legal obligation determined in case law by the courts and set out in legislation.

Compensation for Estate Administration

Executors are entitled to compensation from the estate, if they wish to claim it. The size of compensation depends on the size and complexity of the estate. The guideline for compensation is generally determined by the court in its judgment of the size and complexity of the estate. A small management fee may also be claimed.

Bequests and Legacies

How you wish to pass on your assets is a very personal decision. For some, a simple distribution without restriction to their spouse, and then to their children or next of kin is enough. Some wish to leave more detailed instructions and divisions. What's your stance? Are your children entitled to all you have? Or do you want to provide them only with what they'll need for a successful life and give the rest to charity? Do you want to pass things on "in-kind," as they are—a ring to a niece and a car to a nephew, for example? Or should everything be turned into cash legacies?

Here are some considerations:

• household and personal items: The dispersal of such items can be left to the discretion of your executors, or you can require them to deliver specific items to particular beneficiaries. You can maintain a list and leave it with your will, with a moral, but not legal, obligation for your executors to comply;

• gifts of money: Are you sure there'll be enough money to cover each gift after payment of your debts, estate costs, taxes, etc.? Consider giving a percentage of the residue of the estate instead;

• gifts of specific assets: What happens if you sell or give away the property before you die? Will there be no gift? In that case, would you want the estate to replace the gift with its value, or another asset?

- charitable gifts: A testamentary gift may enable you to support a cause with moneys that were not available when you were alive. You may wish to leave a legacy or remembrance in the form of a donation.

Family Law Issues

The longer a person lives, the greater the chance of a second or even third marriage, following either the death of a spouse or a divorce. The resulting family ties should be considered in planning your estate, particularly if there are children, adult or otherwise.

Upon remarriage, any pre-existing will should be revised to ensure that the testator's estate distribution is conducted according to their current wishes.

Prenuptial Agreements

It's sometimes difficult to talk with a loved one about the need for a prenuptial agreement (a contract made before marriage to deal with matters such as ownership of assets, support obligations, etc.), mainly in the case of a second marriage. Later in life, it's prudent and can alleviate problems and discord, not only in the case of a breakdown of the second marriage, but also in the case of death. A prenuptial agreement is particularly desirable where a person has accumulated a substantial estate and wishes to protect the interests of their children.

Through the terms of a contract prepared in contemplation of marriage, obligations can be created that will not be terminated on death. They will, in effect, create a debt of the estate to be dealt with by the executor along with other liabilities left by the deceased.

Family Law Obligations

While the specific legislation may vary from state to state, obligations regarding the support of dependants are standard. If you have supported someone (normally a child or spouse, or another individual who has grown dependent on your support), the obligation to continue the support will survive your death. As with certain terms in a prenuptial agreement, these obligations bind your estate and the dependant will be entitled to continued support as long as your estate has the assets to pay.

Even where legislation has not specifically dealt with support or property obligations, legal duties can arise.

> Martin had a niece who'd given up a well-paying job to live with him and care for him for many years. He had told her many times not to worry about her future because he would look after her in his will and leave her a good income and the house. He died without mentioning her in his will and with no other documentation to this effect.

In this scenario, Martin's niece has a very good chance of enforcing her claim in a court action for support and perhaps for the house as well.

It's vitally important to properly plan your estate and set in place valid Powers of Attorney and a will. It's easy to procrastinate; it can be difficult to face your own vulnerability and mortality. But you'll be relieved once the task is done.

Being prepared for your initial consultation with your lawyer will save both time and money and help to ensure that your needs are met. In Appendix B, "Preparing to Meet Your Advisors," there are checklists to help plan for your meeting with your lawyer.

7

The
Final Exit

Spas are booming, the food industry designs ever more "healthy" products, and vitamin pills are consumed enthusiastically, all with these goals in mind: to feel better and live longer. But no one can avoid death, no matter how much time and money they spend fighting the forces of nature.

Many prefer not to talk about death. Some cultural communities even consider it a death wish on the part of an individual if he or she pre-arranges his or her own funeral.

But today's advertisers emphasize the necessity of planning for the day we're separated from our loved ones. Benjamin Franklin's words, "In this world nothing can be said to be certain, except death and taxes," have become a mainstay of advertising firms marketing funeral products and services. Insurance companies with celebrity spokespeople, talk openly about the importance of leaving something behind for your family or how to avoid burdening your loved ones with funeral costs.

One advertiser used a symphony orchestra to compare a simple funeral to one with all the bells and whistles.

Tasteless as some of this may be, it's nonetheless true that it is essential to plan in advance for your own death. This chapter explains various aspects of the funeral process.

The end-of-life ceremonies, rituals and traditions of each culture and faith, reflect essential spiritual beliefs and other values. In your decisions, you will no doubt draw on your own traditions. The material below contains material relevant to final life-stage planning. It begins with cremation and earth burial, among the most ancient and widely practiced ways of taking care of human remains.

Cremation

Cremation, or the incineration of the body, is the exclusive practice in some religions, and may be chosen in others.

To arrange for cremation, after death, the next of kin or legal representative of the deceased must give cremation authorization to a licensed funeral director. Often, families call the cemetery directly to engage the services of a crematorium. But cemeteries are not permitted to complete the cremation application and registration of death; these must be done by a licensed funeral establishment or transfer service.

Some religions such as Judaism require burial to take place the following day after death.

In religious communities where there is a strict and defined time cremation must take place after death, it is up to the funeral director and a coroner appointed by the state to sign the cremation application along with the executor appointed by the deceased. Once signed by the coroner, the cremation may begin immediately.

In some cases, when a death occurs, the family and executor must decide between cremation and burial. The choice might not be easy.

"We talked to Dad during his illness and he said he wanted to be cremated. We wanted to fulfill Dad's wishes, but were concerned that if we had a cremation, we wouldn't be able to have a funeral."

Cremation does not eliminate the funeral and the value the funeral provides. In a recent study, Batesville Caskets, a leading distributor of funeral merchandise to funeral homes in North America, confirmed that families cremating their loved ones have the same bereavement needs as those burying their loved ones, including a strong need to say goodbye.

After Cremation

The cremation process usually takes two or three hours to complete. Cremated remains are placed in a container constructed of hard plastic. The cremated remains can remain in this container permanently, or an urn can be purchased from a funeral home or cemetery. Affixed to the cremated remains is a cremation certificate with vital information. If you use a cemetery for final interment, you must release the cremation certificate to the cemetery. If you keep the cremated remains indefinitely, you then retain the certificate for your own records.

After cremation, the family has several options for final disposition of the cremated remains, including:

• interment in a cemetery in the family plot, or grave: Most cemeteries allow at least three urns to be placed in one adult-size grave;

• placement in a niche in a columbarium at a cemetery (indoors or outdoors): More churches are constructing niches in churchyards, where members and their families can place cremated remains;

• scattering cremated remains on cemetery grounds: Not all cemeteries permit this or have a designated area in which to scatter remains;

- scattering the cremated remains elsewhere: If you scatter on private property that is not your own, you must receive the permission of the landowner, preferably in writing;
- burial at sea: this is a common practice for former/active military servicemen;
- keep remains in your possession
- interment in common ground at a cemetery: Most cemeteries will inter the cremated remains, for a fee, in a vault with others, in a designated area. The grave is numerically marked. You may not place a marker or headstone on the grave to commemorate your loved one.

Earth Burial

Earth burial is the act of placing a body in a grave or tomb. As with cremation, it is the exclusive practice in some religions, and may be chosen in others.

Before an earth burial can take place, you must own a plot of land at a cemetery. A deed is produced upon purchase of a grave, or graves. This is very similar to a deed produced when purchasing a home. When the grave is needed for burial, only the person stated on the deed can grant permission for the opening. The executor provides the signature of authorization, as well as the designation of which grave to open. All cemeteries can readily provide you with ownership information if a deed has been misplaced or is unavailable.

Burial Vault

Most cemeteries do not require a burial vault. However, if a family chooses to have one, there are two advantages. A vault protects the grave from caving in after the casket is buried, something which usually happens after enduring many years of weight from the packed earth. A lined vault protects the casket from the elements, such as water. The choice of a vault is a personal one. Vaults can be purchased from a funeral home at the time of pre-arranging or arranging a funeral, or from the cemetery.

Caskets and Containers

Funeral homes provide caskets or cremation containers for burial and cremation. A family must choose a casket or container at the time they make the funeral arrangements. There's a wide cross-section of caskets and cremation containers to choose from today. Most funeral homes also provide a number of rental caskets to choose from if the final disposition is cremation.

Funeral Service

For many, their faith and culture will determine the type of funeral service they will have. For others, a variety of ways may be considered appropriate to celebrate a loved one's life, or mark his or her passing.

> "Mom was 93 years old and had outlived most of her friends. She was an intensely private person who didn't want a funeral, but wanted to have her family gather where a few words could be said before the cremation. She particularly wanted the caring chaplain who visited her every day while she was in the hospital to be present."

The experience of losing a friend or family member emotionally affects us in many different ways. Some individuals dread the public interaction after losing a loved one and others are not up to sharing their loss in a public way. Private services with only family members and invited guests may be the best way for them to say their goodbyes. Others may find public outpouring of support from family, friends, and acquaintances the first step in getting through their loss. Hugs, embracing, a good cry, or a gentle touch can be so meaningful to those left behind. Every person responds and copes with death differently. The best form of funeral or ceremony is achieved when families can be together, allowing them to talk about their own emotional needs at the time, and planning for something that will touch each person in a particular way.

Families who choose cremation have the option of using the crematorium chapel, instead of their regular place of worship, to hold their funeral service. The family may or may not want the casket open prior to the service. Upon completion of the funeral service, the cremation process usually begins in an adjacent crematorium.

Memorial Service

A memorial service is usually celebrated after cremation or burial has taken place. It's a celebration of life held in a venue of your choice. The casket is not present, although very often photographs and portraits assist those participating to share memories of the deceased. Whether the cremated remains are present or not is up to the family.

> "After retirement, Dad played the saxophone in a local jazz band. He and his friends in the band played at various fundraisers in the community. At his memorial service, his friends played his favorite music by Gershwin. At the front of the funeral home chapel was Dad's saxophone, on a stand, with a collection of his favorite CDs."

A memorial service can be personalized to a large degree. For example, some families read passages, play music, or display items loved by the deceased.

> "Mom loved her garden. For her service of remem-

brance, we arranged a large bouquet of flowers from her garden and placed it at the front of the church."

A funeral home ran an advertisement that described a personalized memorial gathering organized by a group of golfing friends:

He was diligent when it came to contracts and clients, but on Fridays, he almost always managed to escape his busy practice to play a well-earned 18 holes.

Last Friday, family, friends, and fellow duffers dressed in spikes and polo shirts gathered on the 18th-hole green. They came to share fond memories and swap stories.

A lone piper, silhouetted against the setting sun, provided the score for the thoughtful procession as it headed back down the fairway. They all knew that, from that day forward, whenever they remembered Andrew, they'd think of him on the 18th.

A favorite place...Amazing Grace...a pin flag at half-mast.

Location of the Service

Church Funeral

"Our family has been attending this parish for over 40 years. My kids were confirmed in this church and were eventually married here as well. To have a Mass here would be important to us as a family."

Often, it's appropriate that the funeral should be held at the family church. The casket is brought to the church on the day of the funeral. Flowers, guest register books, and charitable donation cards are set up well before the funeral begins. Some churches today, suggest visitation prior to the funeral, in the church sanctuary or narthex.

If the final disposition is cremation, usually only the funeral home staff journey to the crematorium from the church. However, if family members have a strong desire to see the cremation process begin, called "witnessing," they may go too. Some clerics may wish to go to the crematorium for a final committal prayer.

In some traditions, the funeral service begins in the home and proceeds directly to the cemetery or crematorium. In others, the funeral begins at home, proceeds to a more public place, such as religious premises, then proceeds to the cemetery or crematorium.

If the family chooses burial, then family and friends often go, in a funeral procession from the church, to the cemetery for the burial.

Graveside Service

Families who own a plot of land at a cemetery, sometimes wish to have the funeral and committal services by the grave. Family members, the funeral director, and the cleric meet at the family plot, where a funeral service is conducted. Family may participate in the placement of the cremated remains in the prepared grave at the appropriate time. If it is a burial with a casket, the funeral director will arrange to have the casket placed over the grave before family and friends arrive.

More and more families are asking for this type of service, in all seasons and types of weather. To bring greater formality and comfort to the service, particularly for the frailer mourners, funeral homes and cemeteries can, if requested, put up tents and place chairs around the grave.

Funeral Home Chapel Service

"We grew up attending church regularly, but since we moved away from the family church, many years ago, we haven't attended any church. We don't know a cleric who could conduct my husband's funeral."

The funeral home chapel is used more today than it was decades ago. Families who want a religious funeral, but no longer attend a church, will often use the funeral home chapel. All funeral homes can arrange for a cleric, of almost any denomination, to provide a religious or spiritual service.

"My mother lived to be 94 years of age. She was a member of a church and contributed in many ways for years. However, because of her age, she outlived most of her friends. We, as a family, would feel very uncomfortable if only a dozen people showed up. The church would look empty."

A concern some families feel about a church funeral is, who and how many will show up? Most funeral home chapels are smaller than most church sanctuaries and provide a comfortable setting for a smaller gathering of family and friends. Many funeral homes also provide receptions for friends of the family following the service. When mourners come from a distance and are unfamiliar with the community, it helps if they only have one place to find.

Non-Religious Service

In today's world, some individuals/families do not have any religious affiliation but will still hold a funeral ceremony or celebration honoring the deceased. Those without religious beliefs may request a humanist chaplain (eg., Unitarian) to conduct the service. Humanists relate nature to how we exist in this world. Some families will choose an individual to conduct the service. Attention is given to poetry or eulogies delivered by friends and family with no existential references to life after death. Many services include comedy, music, and quoting from the deceased's favorite books. These aspects are also part of many religious services. Non-religious services may be held in venues other than the church or funeral chapel such as a community hall, local pub, private home, theatre, or art gallery.

Pre-Planning Your Funeral

"I've given my eventual funeral a lot of thought recently, and I want to note my wishes. My children are uncomfortable talking about it, so perhaps I should see a funeral director who handles pre-planning."

Death is a subject many people avoid until they're faced with the responsibility of making arrangements for the disposition of a deceased family member or friend. Pre-planned arrangements spare survivors the burden of having to make detailed, emotional decisions at the time of the funeral arrangement. Most important, planned arrangements ensure that your wishes are fulfilled.

A funeral pre-arrangement can be as simple as noting your wishes in a journal and making these wishes known to a family member, friend, executor, or cleric. The pre-planning process may also include going to a funeral home and meeting with a pre-planning director who can assist you in formalizing your funeral wishes. Pre-planning directors note your funeral wishes and produce an estimate of costs. Pre-arrangements are then filed at the funeral home until services are needed.

Pre-Paying Your Funeral Expenses

"I've allocated a certain amount of my savings to be used to pay for my funeral. I don't want my children to be responsible for the funeral expenses when I die."

Funeral Trust

This is an arrangement between the grantor and funeral home/cemetery to allow for the prepayment of funeral expenses. The funeral trust is a "pooled income fund" set up by a funeral home/cemetery to which a person transfers property to cover future funeral and burial costs. These are grantor trusts, with the grantor responsible for reporting income. The trustee may make an election on qualified pre-need funeral trusts to not be treated as a grantor trust, with the tax being paid by the trustee.

A funeral isn't guaranteed until paid in full. If a person starts paying for his or her funeral in installments and dies before full payment is made, the Estate or family will pay the difference on the total cost of the funeral.

Pre-planning a funeral does not mean you must pre-pay the funeral expenses; this is simply one option. Some families have the money to cover their funeral expenses invested elsewhere and only want to detail the funeral arrangements.

Another way to cover your funeral expenses in advance is through life insurance. This option is being requested more and more today, and there are now fewer eligibility requirements for receiving insurance. Most funeral homes offer some insurance products, and you need not deal with an insurance salesperson directly. Many funeral homes also offer monthly pre-authorized payment plans from checking accounts or credit cards. Check with your particular funeral home.

Even if you have a long-term family relationship with a funeral home, pre-planning is a competitively priced service, and you may wish to explore the options available in your region. If you're planning on behalf of a friend or relative living in another community, you should investigate the services offered there.

A financial advisor can help you consider the options and make the decision that's best for your situation.

You may have many years of life still ahead of you, or your last day may come much sooner than you or your family expect. Planning your funeral in advance ensures that, whenever your life ends, your final wishes will be met and your last gesture to your loved ones will be one of care and consideration.

Part II

Caregiving

8

Being
a Caregiver

Are you sandwiched between your children and parents, or are you a hamburger, layered with children, work, marriage, and aging relatives? Perhaps you've become an empty nester and the world is your oyster when, suddenly, a parent or loved one needs you.

Everyone is familiar with the terms "squeezed" or "sandwiched generation." These are the adult children who are today between the ages of 35 and 65, caught between their own growing children and aging parents, trying to juggle careers, child-rearing, and caregiving. In today's families, there may be as many as four generations in the equation: preschoolers from a second marriage, teenagers or young adults, parents or partners, and seniors.

Never before have so many entered middle age with their parents still alive. With more people living longer, it's not unusual to see 70-year-olds looking after 90-year-old parents.

Whether you're young or old, female or male, whether you work outside the home, are a homemaker, or are retired, caregiving can tax your emotions, take its toll physically, and strain your finances. Just trying to cope can be a tremendous burden.

Are you already a caregiver? About to become one? If not, before you turn to another chapter, think about this: If you aren't a caregiver yet, you may be one sooner than you think. Being informed about this increasingly common role, and planning ahead for it, can save you much distress and misery.

If you are being cared for now, or may soon require care, read this section, too. It will help you understand what your caregiver may be facing and help you make your relationship healthy and productive.

Are You Equipped for Caregiving?

Caregiving may be a role you chose, or it may have chosen you. Either way, take time to consider the information below, which can help you do the best possible job, or to decide that you need more help and more options. In any situation, there are usually more options than at first it may seem.

Attitudes

How do you feel about being old? Are you yourself enjoying growing older? Or does old age frighten or worry you? Do you feel that when someone grows old they are no longer useful or valuable? Do you think most people lose their ability to think clearly and make sound decisions as they age? Attitudes such as these will not only make your own aging more difficult, they will also impair your ability to be a good caregiver.

Do you assume caregiving will be nothing but a burden? Or, while recognizing its challenges, do you see it as an opportunity to build a relationship in a new way, one that can bring new depths of love, respect, compassion, responsibility, and sharing. How it all turns out will have a lot to do with your attitude.

Being Partners

Do you think the needs of the partner who is frail, or those of the one who is not, should be given priority? Do you think that those who work the hardest and pay for the most in the family should have greater rights? Are you afraid that, if you were to raise problems, you'd just seem like a whiner or complainer? Or are you a good partner?

Caregiving is a partnership. Successful partners appreciate one another's strengths even as they are realistic about their weaknesses. They see their partner for who they are, and are tolerant. They respect one another's values. They know the needs and wants of each are equally important; they're open about what they themselves feel and non-judgemental about what the other members of the team may feel. They enjoy helping one another to fulfill their needs. They are committed.

Like all partnerships, caregiving needs good communication, planning, rules, and respect. Miscommunication with others involved, about perceptions and responsibilities, can quickly undermine your best intentions and efforts.

Responsibilities

Are you prepared to shoulder the responsibilities of a caregiver? Do you feel confident that you can handle these responsibilities? Are there some that worry you?

Finances, in particular, must be factored into caregiving and require an open, honest dialogue by the entire family. Not only is caregiving a time-consuming task, it can be very costly. When parents don't have sufficient funds for the necessary care, family members may have to contribute financially. You may love your parents dearly, but love alone will not sustain you. Solicit input from community resources about what government programs are available to seniors when their personal finances don't cover all their needs.

If you or other family members don't presently need care, but anticipate that care may be required in the future, consider acquiring long-term care insurance (see chapter 15).

Being Informed

To be an effective caregiver, you need to be well informed on many topics. The right information can help you provide the best possible care and ease your burden. Reading this book will get you started. Gather further information at your local library, from television shows, and, especially, off the Internet, where you can find not only information, but support. Talk to others, particularly other caregivers, about the challenges you face. Even someone who is not a caregiver can share good ways to manage time, solve problems, and relate to others, or, even better, be a supportive and objective sounding board as you work out your own best plan.

Making Decisions

Every person has the right to be considered in any decisions about what he or she does, with whom, how, and why.

As a caregiver, you may be called on to make important decisions on another person's behalf. You'll need to make sure you never make decisions for another without adequate consultation or consideration of their wishes and well-being. The Golden Rule, "Treat others the way you would like them to treat you," remains fundamental. Remember that what you do *with* others, however young or old, is usually better than what you may do *to* them, or *for* them, without their informed consent.

When facing a decision that needs to be made, ask yourself:

• Who and what in this situation are likely to affect or be affected by my values?

• What information do I need to honor their values?

• How much will my personal attitude affect the outcomes?

• What is the most responsible course to take?

• How can we, together, most courageously and creatively, cooperate and collaborate to make the happiest decisions for the future?

Decisions made in haste, or without another's input, can have sad results, and too often, all the regrets and repentance in the world can't undo all the harmful consequences.

Should the person you're caring for be unable to make decisions for him or herself, it creates special problems. Most countries have laws governing how care is managed when this occurs. It's up to each person to become familiar with his or her own set of circumstances.

Workplace Concerns

Physically, you're at work, but you're spending an inordinate amount of time on the phone trying to secure Meals on Wheels for your mother, or finding a cleaner, or someone to cut the grass. Such demands are one of the reasons many workplaces offer employees senior care resource programs. A good employer knows the value of a good employee. Helping employees become aware of community resources and solutions to common senior care problems can enable them to remain productive, so everyone benefits.

What is the situation at your workplace? Find out what your company's policies and practices are in such situations. Talk frankly to your employer about what adjustments may be possible. It's much better to plan in advance than to have to suddenly tell your boss you won't be able to make tomorrow's important presentation to a key client because you have to deal with a caregiving issue. The responsible approach is to anticipate the problem and have a backup plan.

Don't forget that your caregiving demands may result in new costs for your employer too. You want your employer to be sympathetic and supportive; start by being that way yourself. What impact might your absences or interruptions (time on the phone), or your distractedness and exhaustion, have on your performance and productivity?

You may also wish to explore with your employer an option such as flex-time, job-sharing, reducing your hours (and income) a bit, or arranging to work from home as a way to relieve some of your work pressure.

Stress

How good are you at handling stress? "Burnout" is a frequent problem for caregivers. Burnout can stem from fatigue, conflicting demands, financial concerns, and changes in daily routine and recreation. Burnout can occur not only at home, but on the job as well. Each person, every day, is faced with stressful situations, but if you place too much stress on yourself, your body can't cope.

Too much stress and lack of sleep can lead to depression. You may feel engulfed in an unhappy situation you can't see your way out of. Don't feel guilty about feeling discouraged or down. It's completely natural; no one is able to stay happy all the time, particularly when overburdened with responsibilities. A good therapist can make a major difference. He or she can help you understand your feelings and figure out ways to handle difficult situations. It can be wise to begin a relationship with a counselor before you really need to. Having someone outside the situation to talk to, will help relieve stresses before they become extreme, and if a real crisis hits, your support is ready and waiting. Some agencies have trained telephone counselors who'll listen and offer suggestions on specific concerns. They may even be fellow caregivers.

When caregiving is really getting you down:

• try to figure out what *specifically* is bothering you (no time to yourself, no one to talk to about how you feel, etc.) and what you can do about it;

• find someone empathetic to talk to (a friend, relative, therapist, cleric, etc.);

• do something you enjoy doing with the person you're caring for (playing cards, taking a walk, etc.);

• do something you really like to do to cheer yourself up. Indulge yourself somehow;

• take care of yourself;

• have a good laugh. It'll make you feel better;

• consider using meditation or yoga to reduce stress;

• get professional help if you need it;

Look back over the list you made of things you want to change in your life plan. Can you alleviate some stresses?

Get organized. Make lots of lists. Rank everything 1, 2, and 3 in terms of how important it is, then work on getting the 1s done. You may occasionally get a 2 done, but don't be surprised if you never get to the 3s. A wise time manager lets lots of things fall through the cracks. If nothing did, it would mean you were paying the same amount of attention to everything, and not prioritizing. Likely, you would not really be giving the important things the attention they deserve. The best part is, if you ignore things long enough (except the really important things), often either someone else does them or they cease to matter.

Feelings Related to Caregiving

The issues surrounding caregiving can evoke many different feelings, depending on the relationship between the caregiver and the person being cared for. An estranged family member may be riddled with anger, frustration, and irritability at the idea of having to pitch in and care for a senior. The martyr will offer a dutiful, loving, joyful face to the world, but in fact may be suffering from fatigue and feel trapped in the role. The adult child who's always enjoyed a pleasant, close relationship with his or her parents will likely be happy to help them, be generous in giving, and will want to stay involved as long as possible. Some will find themselves caregivers to an elderly aunt or uncle, caught in a web of decision-making around healthcare and housing for someone they may know little about.

Some will roll up their sleeves, take action, do what needs to be done, and end up feeling exploited; others will volunteer little if any help, then complain about being kept out of the loop. Resentment can build quickly.

Caregiving can be a monumental task for family members, especially if the burden falls primarily on one set of shoulders. A parent may have a strong preference for which child will look after him or her, and it will not always be the best solution for either of them. The chosen adult child may not have the necessary time to devote to meeting the care needs of the parent, or he or she may live far away, creating unnecessary travel and loss of work time.

Parents can exacerbate such feelings by laying guilt on their adult children: "Why don't you visit me more often?" You may find yourself making excuses not to visit your mom or dad, simply to avoid hearing all her or his woes. "You never call me," really just means, "You don't call me as often as I'd like you to." Try to listen for what's really being said and not feel defensive and angry—or guilty—when another uses this kind of unfair tactic.

To avoid encouraging unrealistic expectations, set up clear ground rules. How often you will be able to visit? Who will be responsible for what? When and what time and money will you will be able to contribute? Communication is always better when everyone knows clearly what to expect. Rules will also provide a good framework for discussion if needs change and adaptations need to be made.

Some will find themselves caring for a senior who's so critical, dissatisfied, negative, irritable, irascible, or self-centered, that he or she has driven off even the most patient friends and kindly neighbors. If this type of behavior is new, it may have a medical cause; get the individual to their doctor for a thorough check-up. But some people seem to like being unpleasant, and if the person you're caring for has always been this way, it's unlikely they'll change now. This doesn't mean you have to accept their behavior. Don't feel obliged to spend time with someone who doesn't treat you well. Tell them you won't do anything unessential for them, or stay to keep them company, until they shape up. In particular, if such a senior lives with you and you find they're undermining your own mental health, it's time to look for another option.

Coping with Anger and Frustration

No one should ever be expected to put up with bad treatment. Though abuse can occur in an institutional or public care setting, seniors can also fall victim to abuse from family members. This abuse may be physical, emotional, or financial. It may result from neglect rather than violence; some seniors face extreme isolation, hunger, or inadequate heat, clothing, or hygiene.

Victims of abuse at the hands of relatives and loved ones often feel ashamed or blame themselves for the problem. Seniors who rely upon their caregivers for help can be very reluctant to blow the whistle, for fear of reprisal or heightened conflict. Caregivers who have difficulty coping with the responsibilities of caregiving in a healthy way, urgently need support.

Almost everyone loses his or her temper once in a while, and everyone is entitled to an occasional bad day. Caregiving can be extremely stressful, and it's understandable if you occasionally lose it. Forgive yourself; guilt can just make you feel angrier. Then, apologize to the person you yelled at. Next time you feel anger mounting, try to remove yourself from the situation right away. You may just need to spend a few minutes alone in another room. Calm yourself with a cup of tea or a walk. This technique will get easier and easier as you practice it.

Yelling a lot, however, is a danger sign, and can escalate to physical violence. On its own, it can cause emotional harm. If you think you may be at risk for abusing a senior, or have done so, to your regret, get the professional help you need to deal with your difficult situation. Talk to your doctor or cleric, or to another helping professional such as a psychologist or family counselor. Also, consider other possible options for caregiving. You may have done all you can for now.

If you're being abused, tell someone you trust about the situation. They'll help you to decide how best to approach it. But do something! By doing something you will get help for yourself and the abuser, who also needs help.

Family Involvement

> When Tim's mother became physically weak and required placement in a care facility, she quite bluntly told Tim that she preferred to have Ruth, Tim's first wife, look after her needs. Ruth and Tim's mother had developed a long-term, comfortable relationship. Tim's current wife was a newcomer in his mother's life. Thus, the caregiving role fell to Ruth, who had to take charge, relegating Tim to a lesser role in his mother's care.

You may be the most obvious person to take care of your elderly relative, but are you the right person? If not, who would be best?

Frequently, the role of caring for a senior will fall to one specific person in a family. When that's you, try to involve other siblings or close relatives in the care planning.

To make important family decisions, hold family meetings and create agendas. Let everyone talk and make decisions together. If that proves impossible, hire an objective third party as a facilitator (see chapter 5).

If you're stuck with too large a burden, don't just complain, but not do anything about it. Call a family meeting. Explain your feelings calmly. Discuss in concrete terms what's become too much for you to cope with, and how it's affecting you and your life. Divide up the duties more fairly. Some jobs, no one will want; take turns with these.

Talk about who'll take over if you become sick, have to travel on business, or have another family emergency of some kind to deal with.

Form a partnership with another relative, or form a team with everyone who's willing to help. Don't just delegate jobs; work together to manage the situation.

Also, don't forget the impact your caregiving may have on your own family. Keep your spouse, partner, or children in the loop about what you're dealing with. Let them know how they can help you. Encourage them to tell you if they feel their own needs aren't being met. Then, together, you can figure out what to do.

The Family and Medical Leave Act of 1993
Public Law 103-3
Enacted 2/5/1993

The FMLA is to grant family and temporary medical leave under certain circumstances. An eligible employee shall be entitled to a total of 12 workweeks of leave during any 12-month period for one or more of the following:

• Because of the birth of a son or daughter of the employee and in order to care for such son or daughter.
• Because of the placement of a son or daughter with the employee for adoption or foster care.
• In order to care for the spouse, or a son, daughter, or parent, of the employee, if such spouse, son, daughter, or parent has a serious health condition.

• Because of a serious health condition that makes the employee unable to perform the functions of the position of such employee.

An employer may require that a request for leave be supported by a certification issued by the health care provider of the eligible employee or of the son, daughter, spouse, or parent of the employee, as appropriate. Any eligible employee who takes leave for the intended purpose of the leave shall be entitled, on return from such leave:

• To be restored by the employer to the position of employment held by the employee when the leave commenced; or
• To be restored to an equivalent position with equivalent employment benefits, pay, and other terms and conditions of employment.

The employer may require an employee on leave to report periodically to the employer on the status and intention of the employee to return to work.

Taking Care of Yourself

To be an effective caregiver, you have to know how to take care of yourself. Caregiving can be a daunting task. Keeping ahead of the issues will help ward off stress and burnout, but you must also recognize the importance of meeting your own needs.

Solicit help from siblings, friends, or neighbors when the tasks at hand become overwhelming. An only child may need to look to outside sources. If respite care is offered, either through a government agency or in the private sector, take advantage.

Caregivers often neglect themselves more than they realize. Make sure to eat properly, exercise regularly, and take time for yourself—at least 20 minutes a day—to listen to a favorite CD, read a magazine, have coffee or a phone date with a friend, take a leisurely walk, or linger in the bath. If you can't manage an evening out, rent a movie and watch it in three installments. Don't just try to keep your sense of humor, look for the humor in life. Laughter is great medicine.

Get extra help just for you. You need to free up new time to compensate for the time you spend caregiving. Many of the strategies that can help individuals stay independent as they age, can also keep you from burnout when you're a caregiver. Find services that can save time on your own shopping, cooking, cleaning, laundry, and daily travel, then avail yourself of all you can afford.

If you have too much to do and not enough time to do it, you'll simply have to stop doing some things, unless you can find more time or someone else to do them. Remind yourself of the things that are most important to you. This could mean having time for coffee with a friend, but in a rather messy kitchen, or maybe your dream is to sit quietly having coffee alone, reading a magazine. Cut back on less-important chores wherever you can. Think about what you can skip, do less often, or differently. Even just ordering pizza once a week instead of making dinner can help.

If a relative or friend asks what he or she can do to help, don't just think of what they could do for the person you're caring for. Ask yourself, what could they do for *me?* For example, perhaps they could take your kids on an expedition to the museum or zoo, or get your Christmas tree, while you have a very, very long bath, with ridiculous amounts of bath foam, then get into a freshly made bed, in the middle of the afternoon, with a magazine or novel, and a bowl of super-rich-triple-everything ice cream. *Mmmmmm.* This is the sort of thing a friend can do for you.

This having been said, don't let advice from others get you down. It's easy to feel like a failure when you're being bombarded by what sounds like good advice, but when you try it, things don't seem to get better, or you never even have the time or energy to try a new approach to a problem. Remember, your situation is not exactly like anyone else's. There are common dilemmas faced by caregivers, but many things in your situation may be unique.

Are you trying to solve too many problems at once? Try to work on one problem at a time. Start with a small one, not the largest. It'll increase your chances of success, which will give you new energy to tackle a slightly bigger problem.

Do you think you have all the answers? Attending a caregiver support group will give you an opportunity to share, with others in the same situation, ways and means of coping with the demands of caring for a older loved one.

> Karin, a nurse, felt that, as a professional, she could handle caring for her elderly mother without help. When prodded by her own doctor to find a support group, she was relieved to learn she was not alone.

To get some time for yourself, you may need to place your loved one in a care facility while you take a vacation from caregiving. Short stays, of anywhere from one to four weeks, are possible in many places, giving you an opportunity to go away, or stay at home to do all the things you haven't had time for. If you explain your needs to the person you're caring for before embarking on securing the proper respite for him or her, it'll be better for both of you.

> Ernest's son and daughter take turns caring for him. He lives in his daughter Monica's home. When Monica needs a breather, her brother, Rolf, moves into her house while she goes to his home in another city. That way, they help each other.

The best solution is the one that will work for the senior, without causing undue stress to you, the caregiver.

If you have an elderly parent or relative and are not yet facing the caregiving role, assume that you'll do so in the future. Don't wait to be caught by surprise; plan ahead. Then, when the situation presents itself, you'll be ready.

Before a crisis hits, sit down and discuss what you'll do. Ask your parents to make their wishes clear and to execute Powers of Attorney for personal care and finances, to ensure their wishes are met if they become unable to run their lives. A fall or unexpected medical event or diagnosis, can cause life to change course rapidly.

Be prepared.

9

Providing Care

For many, the issue of caregiving isn't a matter of if, it's a matter of when and how. You want to provide the best possible care. Each person and family must determine for themselves how best to do this.

Identifying Age-Related Changes

You ask your mother why she's stopped going to church and her response is, "The minister mumbles." Perhaps she's experiencing hearing loss. Her doctor can ascertain if an audiology test is warranted.

Reading road signs while driving at night becomes more difficult. A trip to the ophthalmologist will help identify if there's a loss of vision and whether a new prescription is needed.

A couple of falls in quick succession may indicate the need for a senior to use a cane or walker. Loss of memory can be another sign of aging.

One of the first changes you may observe in a senior is increasing dependency. The phone rings at work and a familiar voice asks, "Honey, could you bring me a quart of milk on your way home from work?" When such requests occur on a regular basis, they may indicate a need for attention, related specifically to aging. While your parent or relative may not be ready to admit it openly, he or she is beginning to need help. He or she still wants to be independent, and is independent in some ways, but is growing dependant in others.

As people acquire the common diseases of old age, they may neglect to eat properly and become victims of the "tea and toast" syndrome, resulting in an electrolyte imbalance. This may lead to symptoms of dementia that can be corrected with good nutrition. Many other health problems are caused, or exacerbated by, poor nutrition.

Another often-overlooked condition that can be confused with dementia in the elderly, is depression. Depression is an illness that affects an individual's general well-being. It can occur at any time, for no apparent reason, or from adverse life circumstances, such as loss of independence, moving, or the loss of a spouse. Fortunately, it is treatable. When depression is suspected, a doctor should be seen as soon as possible.

How to Cope

• Develop an open line of communication: Talk with your parent or relative about what's happening. Don't patronize and don't talk in platitudes. It won't work. Remember, no one likes to have to admit he or she is growing frail; sympathetic understanding will win cooperation much faster than cajoling. Try to explain your concerns about aging issues using real situations.

• Together, as a family, assess the senior's needs: Encourage other family members to meet with you and your parent or relative to determine what needs he or she has at present, and set up a plan of action in the event of a crisis. (See "Assessing Needs" below.)

• Decide who will be the primary caregiver: You may have no choice in this. But if there is a choice, and if this has not been decided, you need to make this decision together with the senior and other family members.

• Empower the senior to make his or her own choices: A person's responsibility and right to make his or her own decisions, should end only when he or she is no longer competent to make such decisions. Encourage the person you're caring for to be proactive about, and involved in, making decisions. Respect and support his or her decisions, with the proviso that they must be reasonable and realistic for the caregivers, as well as the senior.

• Take care of yourself: You must balance your own needs, and those of your immediate family, with those of the person you're caring for.

• Be realistic about the situation: Recognize that the best and most feasible plan will depend on the amount of time the senior is likely to need the care, and the extent of care required.

Assessing Needs

Ask yourself:

• Can the senior handle shopping for necessities? Can he or she get around on public transportation?

• Does the senior eat well? Take a look inside the refrigerator. Is it empty? If full, is the food still good? Is the senior still able to prepare his or her own meals?

• Is the senior on medication? Check if medications have been taken correctly.

• Can the senior handle housekeeping?

• Are any pets being taken care of adequately?

• Does the senior go out? Is he or she involved in groups or community life?

• If there are piles of unread newspapers, magazines, and unopened mail, could the senior be suffering from depression? Memory loss?

• Does the senior have bruises? These probably indicate falls.

• Is there a strong smell of urine when you open the door? This is a clear indicator of incontinence.

Simple tasks such as shopping, meal preparation, and basic housekeeping (laundry and housecleaning), and the ability to use a telephone and drive or take public transportation, are fundamental requirements for independent living. If you find the senior is unable to do some of these, the first step is to secure services—informal or formal—to help extend independence, make their life easier to manage, and ensure their basic needs are met.

For example, arrange for delivery of groceries (if the senior can still prepare food) or set up Meals on Wheels, to ensure they are getting proper nourishment. Locate a cleaning service and set up automatic bill payments. Check into a local senior's club or adult day center that provides the type of programs that might be enjoyable. If going out is not possible, try to find a volunteer visitor who can make house calls.

When a senior can no longer perform the six basic ADL's (activities of daily living)—bathing, grooming, dressing, eating, getting in and out of bed, and going to the bathroom (continence)—it's time to seek help.

Informal Support Systems

If you can find others to help you with caregiving, it can help you to avoid feeling resentment toward a dependent senior and also guard against burnout. As care needs escalate, the amount of work can become daunting. Could someone else help transport them to and from medical appointments, or accompany them to the bank? Grass cutting or snow shoveling can be major tasks; can they perhaps be done by someone in the neighborhood? Helpers can be young or old; a best friend in their building or neighborhood may be a much younger person.

Informal support systems can provide:
- companionship;
- physical care;
- meal delivery;
- help with household tasks;
- help with shopping;
- transportation;
- home repair and maintenance.

Potential informal support systems include:
- other family members;
- friends and neighbors;
- volunteers from service clubs, or from a religious organization to which the senior belongs.

These are usually all unpaid workers.

Never underestimate the value of friends and neighbors in helping to look after your elderly relative, especially if he or she has lived in the same neighborhood for a long period of time and built strong relationships there.

Bianca traveled from Florida to her mother's hometown to arrange for her placement in a retirement home. Bianca felt that 92-year-old Oriana was too old to be on her own. To her surprise, Bianca discovered that Oriana had a whole network of people who genuinely cared about her. The children of single mothers often came to her apartment until their mothers came home. In exchange, the mothers shopped for Oriana, prepared casseroles for her, or had her to dinner in their apartments. She had all the friends and support she needed. Bianca went back to Florida satisfied that her mother was in good hands.

Do be realistic, however, about what friends, neighbors, and volunteers can do. When someone isn't being paid, there are real limits to how much it's fair to ask, or wise to expect. Be sure to have Plan B ready for the day or month when your volunteer is no longer able to help. Don't leave a volunteer in charge of any task where failure to perform, could have disastrous results. For example, don't put an unqualified volunteer in charge of administering medications. Don't give a neighbor access to personal banking information.

Formal Support Systems

Formal support systems include:
- nurses (public health and visiting);
- personal care aides;
- physical and occupational therapists;
- speech and language pathologists;
- social workers;
- doctors;
- geriatric care managers;
- healthcare agencies;
- hospitals;
- long-term care facilities.

The formal care system involves acute care in a hospital, ongoing care in a long-term care facility, or care at home, delivered by professional healthcare and social service workers. In home care, the personal physician is in charge. Many seniors resist going into a long-term care facility and prefer to remain at home with appropriate services brought to them, from either the public or private sector.

At 85, Anita was diagnosed with cancer and given three to four months to live. She and her husband had lived in the same apartment building for many years, and she had remained there after his death, 15 years before. They had no children, and the year before Anita was diagnosed, her only sister died, leaving her without any close family. However, she was not without help; two much younger individuals whom she had befriended and whom she regarded as "her family" assisted her with basic chores—grocery shopping, replacing a light bulb, going to the mall—and offered her a very special friendship that grew over the years. When her lawyer recognized that Anita needed a professional to manage her care, he referred her to a geriatric-care management group, which developed a care plan for her. She had attentive caregivers around the clock, nourishing meals, and companionship. At first, Anita was able to direct her own care; as she became less and less able to do so, the care management team took charge for her, and Anita was able to die at home in peace and dignity. The friends continued to visit Anita until her death and gave her the camaraderie they had always shared in the past.

If professional healthcare workers are needed, you may wish to consider private-sector services. In the US, there are many government services for seniors, but these services are often overtaxed, and the specific service you need may not be available. It may be desirable to hire workers to fill gaps in care needs. Private healthcare agencies can provide a multitude of types of workers, from drivers to nurses, therapists, and speech pathologists.

Local governments do provide home-care services, and social workers and nurses can make home visits, but many clients find a lack of continuity in personnel and inadequate frequency of contact. Home-care agencies have many needs to meet, limited resources, and stringent regulations under which they may practice. These constraints often leave seniors with less than desirable aid, although the best that government home care can provide.

Locating Support Services

Local Community Information Center

Most major cities publish a directory of community services. They also offer telephone assistance in locating community resources. Many of these are not-for-profit enterprises. They can usually be found under government services in the telephone book.

State Sponsored Senior Insurance Counseling Programs

Most states have senior insurance counseling programs that have been approved by the Commissioner of Insurance or other state regulatory agencies.

Government Services

Often, there are separate sections in local telephone books that list government senior services in a specific location.

Phone Book & Yellow Pages

If you're looking for an agency that will provide homemaking services, or you want a caregiver, look under nurses or the seniors' section. Maybe all you need is a podiatrist for foot problems. The Yellow Pages of the phone book can help you find everything from a retirement home to someone to run errands, or take care of a garden.

The Internet

The Internet is an excellent way of locating resources. Be aware that what you find on the Net is not always accurate information; try to stick to reputable sources such as established not-for-profit organizations and government sites.

Consulting Services

Geriatric care mangers have been a mainstay in the United States for many years. These are qualified nurses, social workers, and psychologists who have training in gerontology and are able to assist families in dealing with all aspects of senior care. If your elderly parent or relative wants to stay at home, have him or her link up with a knowledgeable person familiar with the community and its resources. When staying at home is no longer viable, that same person can assist the senior and you in making the right choice in housing to meet the senior's changing needs.

Hiring Staff

Choosing an agency to provide care to a senior may be the only option open to you. Everyone has unique needs, and to secure the right individual takes time and energy. When a senior requires care, it may be due to a crisis situation and your choices may be limited; you may be forced to accept whoever the agency sends you.

Whatever your plan, in choosing a caregiver, remember that there are no easy answers. The caregiver must be qualified, caring, and a good fit with the person he or she will be caring for; consider personalities. To the fullest extent possible, involve your parent or relative in making the choice.

Agency personnel range from sitter/companions to registered nurses. A senior most frequently requires someone who can prepare meals, assist with personal hygiene, and offer companionship.

If the agency you choose sends someone you don't feel is appropriate or compatible, inform the supervisor; he or she will arrange to have that person replaced.

Senior Abuse

Any harm done to a senior, be it physical, emotional, or financial, is considered a crime against the elderly. Many think senior abuse only happens to incompetent seniors; however, anyone who must rely on others to assist him or her with basic needs—such as shopping or banking—can become a victim. It may even be caused by a trusted source; a family member, friend, or caregiver.

Even when a case of abuse is suspected, it may go unreported because the senior may refuse to testify in court against the person who committed the crime. The senior often feels powerless to do anything for fear of reprisal. Police forces have begun treating these crimes in a manner that helps both parties. Community Relations Departments want to provide the necessary intervention.

Physical injuries are the easiest to spot. An injury caused by a fall can be misinterpreted as abuse. However, bruising received from a caregiving source may signify abuse. When seniors are seen in emergency rooms, healthcare professionals need to carefully investigate the injuries to determine the actual cause, and decide if an injury was accidental or inflicted by someone else.

Since there is no physical evidence, emotional abuse is harder to understand and detect. People who are verbally abused, will rarely admit that it's happening. The abuse is often only discovered if the person has a trusting relationship with an astute person who spots hidden clues—such as crying, anxiety, and nervousness—and responds to them.

Anyone who has control over a senior's finances is capable of financially abusing the situation. This could be as simple as not giving back change after a shopping expedition. Over time, those small amounts build up. Misuse of trust funds by lawyers, trust officers, and even friends, is another form of abuse. It's imperative that extreme care be taken in appointing a Power of Attorney for finances.

If you suspect someone is abusing your relative, you should:
- get the facts from both parties;
- talk to a trusted source, such as a cleric, lawyer, or doctor;
- as a last resort, speak to the local Police Department to ascertain if it has a Community Relations Division or something similar. For the sake of everyone concerned, you'll want to avoid pressing charges unless absolutely necessary.

Problem Solving

Loneliness

The loss of loved ones is painful. The long-term, trusting relationships that were always there, start to melt away. Forming new relationships isn't always easy. Some ways a senior can reduce loneliness include:
- talking with neighbors and friends;
- joining a seniors' or community center that provides activities, programs, and outings;
- looking into volunteering opportunities;
- becoming an active member of an organization—religious, political, social activist, recreational—whose aims the senior supports.

Finding a New Home

If it's the choice of the senior to remain at home, this can usually be achieved, but it will require planning, adapting, and help. The senior who's capable of making decisions, must understand the necessity of being in a safe and secure environment, and that to do so may require changes. They may not feel up to dealing with the telephone calls and research required to implement change, and may need a caring, understanding person to assist them in evaluating the available choices and making the purchases that will enable them to remain at home.

When is the best time to move to a retirement or nursing

home? If a senior demonstrates a decline in personal hygiene or seems confused, the first thing that may pop into your mind may be, "Let's find a nice retirement home." The task of finding the right place for a senior may fall to you. Armed with your own specific set of values, you may go out visiting those facilities that are appealing to you, with the assumption, "If I like it, so will Mother."

> Tom took his parents to lunch at a new, upscale retirement residence in his hometown, thinking they'd jump at the opportunity to be there. After the tour, Tom's father turned to him and said, "It's a little too rich for my blood." Tom felt hurt. He'd envisioned his parents enjoying these elegant surroundings that were close to his home. He had failed to realize that they had a completely different set of values.

When a senior can't manage in their own home anymore, housing can be a major hurdle. Seniors often resist the possibility of a move. Most people want to stay in a familiar setting, even when they can't manage anymore. There are many, often better, choices available. Each community has its own set of options (see chapter 4).

Dealing with Doctors, Lawyers, and Financial Advisors

What are the ethics and correct approaches to supporting a senior? Ask their doctor, lawyer, and financial advisor. They should be able to tell you how best you can support your relative, what they can do, what you should concern yourself with, and what you should leave to them, your relative, or any legal representatives specified, for example, in a Power of Attorney.

Driving

The possibility of not being able to drive is the biggest threat to some seniors. They may say, "I only travel on side roads now. I never go on the highway" or "I only use the car to get my groceries and go to the dentist and doctor." They've already recognized that they're not as able to drive as they once were and have started to compensate for their deficits. However, they may indeed be dangers on the road.

Should you find that your aging relative's car has a few dents, or the side of the garage has been hit, it may be wise to go for a drive to see for yourself how they handle various situations and their overall ability to operate a motor vehicle. Watch for the following:

- driving at inappropriate speeds;
- making improper lane changes;
- either signaling inappropriately, or not signaling at all;
- navigating turns with difficulty;
- hitting curbs;
- failing to anticipate situations;
- confusing the gas pedal and brake;
- getting lost in familiar territory;
- responding to dangerous situations too slowly;
- parking inappropriately;
- becoming increasingly agitated or irritated when driving.

No one, regardless of age, likes to admit that they are having difficulty driving. Early stroke victims are just as likely to be affected as those with Parkinson's or Alzheimer's disease. When negotiating the terrain of safety, deteriorating abilities, and independence, here are some strategies that can help:

- Ascertain if there is a problem: Not all older drivers are unsafe drivers. Many people drive safely all their lives. Experience and knowledge of good driving practices and skills are the keys to being a safe driver. Perhaps a course in driving skills is all that's needed.

• Don't avoid the issue: Start to discuss the situation as soon as difficulty is apparent. The longer you wait, the more likely the driver is to become defensive and hostile toward the subject.

• Try to secure objective help: DriveABLE, and other computerized programs that determine an individual's abilities to operate a vehicle, coupled with a road driving test, are being introduced in the United States. The results are discussed with the client by the tester, removing responsibility from family members or medical personnel.

• Reduce driving time: Encourage the driver to limit their time behind the wheel, pointing out your concerns without taking away the keys. Discourage driving at night or when road conditions are adverse.

• Make alternative transportation suggestions: These could include getting rides with friends and neighbors, as well as other family members. Agencies in most cities, offer qualified drivers for a nominal fee plus mileage. These can be located through the Yellow Pages.

• If necessary, be firm: Drivers who are not able to react and respond appropriately, are a danger to themselves and others. You may have to tell your elderly parent or relative that they are unfit to operate a motor vehicle. Affirm that you'll report them to the appropriate authorities if they are unwilling to give up driving.

Accentuate the positive. If a driver must stop driving, remind them of how much money they will save by not owning a car—cost of car, gas, maintenance and repairs, insurance, parking fees, parking tickets—and that they will now be able to take pride in not depleting essential fossil fuels and polluting the environment. Share secrets non-drivers already know: while some places are harder to get to without a car, many are easier, cheaper, and faster to get to on public transport, once you factor in the time spent stuck in traffic and finding a parking space. Plus, you get the health benefits of walking short distances and to and from the subway or bus stop. With a light knapsack or satchel, carry your reading or knitting on the bus, or just enjoy watching the people. Unless you're traveling to work, you can travel at non-peak times; it won't be crowded and you'll always get a seat. It's much more relaxing and less stressful than dealing with traffic, bad drivers, and road rage.

Creating a Safe Environment

Falls are the leading cause of injuries in people age 65 and over and often a sign of unrecognized health problems. They can lead to loss of independence for seniors and more stress for caregivers. For tips on creating a safe and secure home environment, see chapter 4.

Distance Caregiving

Joyce lives on the West Coast. Her father, Stuart, lives on the East Coast. One day, Joyce had a call from Stuart's partner: her father had driven his car too close to an off-ramp on a highway, hit an abutment, and caused severe damage to the car, then simply walked away. Another driver found the car and called the police, who were able to determine the owner and visited Stuart at home. He had no recollection of the event. Joyce was panic-stricken. This was the first she'd heard of any memory problems in her father. She'd visited him only a couple of months before, and he seemed fine at the time. Now, she had to find a retirement home where Stuart could receive the care he required. Joyce had an understanding boss; he allowed her the necessary time off to return to the East Coast to deal with her family issues.

Today, family members often live great distances from one another, in other cities, on the other side of the country, even an ocean or two away. When you start recognizing that a loved one is showing signs of frailty, whether physical or mental, this separation can lead to great frustration and anxiety. If families don't have the time or means to travel regularly to check on loved ones, substantial challenges can be associated with distance caring.

First, discuss things with your relative and find out their needs and desires. It'll be immensely frustrating, and unnecessary, to go to a huge amount of work to find a nursing home for your parent, only to have them reject your decision, or accept it only under duress.

How do you access local services in a senior community when that community is far away? Publicly funded agencies can link up across the country to process long-term care applications and ensure health insurance coverage continuity for clients, but consistent, single-contact assistance may not be available. This creates difficulties for many seniors and their families who have to make a multitude of telephone calls or write and send many faxes, e-mails, or letters, and interface with strangers at each juncture.

During a visit with her elderly mother Dionne, who lived in another city, Jamila was concerned to see the grass needed cutting and the house was in general disrepair. It had been several months since her last visit, but she'd maintained regular contact by telephone and Dionne sounded fine. Now, Jamila saw that Dionne was not eating properly and had lost her enthusiasm for living. She quickly made an appointment for Dionne to see the family doctor, who mentioned he'd not seen Dionne for some time. After a thorough examination, the doctor determined that Jamila's mother had mild depression that could probably be controlled with medication. Prior to returning home, Jamila arranged for a local agency to visit Dionne regularly and assist with cooking, cleaning, and laundry. The medication worked and Dionne is once again happily involved in all the activities of daily living.

Creating a network of alternative assistance can ensure that seniors and their families have the services they need, when they need them, and a friendly concerned person, not governed by the territorialism or regulatory constraints public sector agencies often have to operate under, with whom they can consult for objective opinions.

The most difficult situation can be when loved ones live in another country. Occasional trips back home don't serve seniors well. Are there still family members nearby who can be counted on if a crisis strikes? If you're an only child, it's even more important to solicit the help of friends and neighbors from your parent or relative's community. Depression and memory loss may not be apparent in a telephone call.

Failing that, when you do visit a senior who lives far away, watch carefully for warning signs of an impending crisis (see Assessing Needs, above).

After visiting her parents in England, Deirdre realized they were beginning to show signs of decline. No siblings lived nearby, but after a bit of digging, she tracked down a cousin who lived within a half-hour of her parents. He was willing to be available to help in a crisis and agreed to make regular telephone calls and visits to her parents.

Great distances can be bridged with telephone calls. More and more seniors are on the Internet and have access to e-mail. Grandchildren often use this method of communication when their grandparents are in another city. This can be an easy and effective way to maintain daily contact with seniors, even when they only live across town.

Letter writing is almost a forgotten art. How exciting it is to find a personal letter in the mailbox. Think of how happy it would make a senior who lives in another part of the world, to find a letter he or she could touch, read and reread as often as he or she wanted. This is true contact with a loved one.

The following are suggestions if you're caring for a senior who doesn't live near you.

• Have a neighbor or trusted friend maintain contact with your relative and keep you informed of any significant changes that may warrant a visit. If you live out of town, a visit from a friendly neighbor can help relieve loneliness.

• Keep handy pertinent information on your relative: insurance and health card numbers, phone numbers for doctors, dentists, hospitals, caregivers, and the landlord as well as a list of medications. Know where wills and Powers of Attorney can be found if needed. This information must be kept current.

• Have a logbook at your relative's home to track medications, doctor and dental appointments, and support visits from people such as a house cleaner or gardener (including their telephone numbers).

• Keep a list of agencies in your relative's community that you can call upon if care is needed.

Caring for someone else, or arranging for care, is never easy, but the challenges can be reduced significantly by using problem-solving strategies and availing yourself of any and all supports and services you can. This will reduce your worries and, especially if you're the primary caregiver, leave you more time and energy to refresh yourself, which will make it easier to enjoy and appreciate the person you're caring for.

What is a Geriatric Care Manager

A geriatric care manager is a professional who specializes in helping older adults, their families and friends with senior care concerns. They have extensive training in gerontology, nursing, social work, or psychology, have compassion towards seniors and are knowledgeable about community resources.

A geriatric care manager will:

• Identify existing problems with an in-depth consultation to determine the older person's specific needs and provide a full comprehensive care plan to the client and family.

• Arrange for services and resources to be brought into the home so the person may remain there as long as possible.

• Refer to specialists in geriatrics, psychiatry or other medical and health related services.

• Be an advocate for the older person, more specifically when family members do not live close by.

• Provide on-going education and support to the client and their family.

• Assist with choosing and moving to an alternate living arrangement when required, such as a retirement or nursing home that best meets the senior's needs.

Choose a geriatric care manager wisely and carefully. The field is relatively unregulated and many without qualifications or specific training identify themselves as care managers, case managers, or care advisors. By screening the prospective candidate, you can determine if you are working with a person qualified in this new profession by:

Inquiring into their training and education and length of time they have worked in the field of gerontology. Ask if they hold a university degree or belong to a professional organization.

Ask how responsive they are to client needs. How do they handle emergencies? What sort of backup do they have when off duty or away from work? Are they part of an agency or are they a private consultant?

What experience have they had in the field of gerontology? Aside from providing the initial interview, consultation and report, do they do continuing on-going care management? Can they meet your specific needs?

Do they subscribe to your philosophy of care for the senior?

Can they work with those who are already involved in caring for the senior?

Ask for letters of reference or names of previous clients you may contact.

Ask if they are certified in gerontology and from what institution?

Find out exactly their billing procedure. Fees may vary depending on location, private or public agency, private practice, contractual or hourly billing.

A geriatric care manager should be able to answer all your questions and concerns. This is a very personal experience and needs to be one that is comfortable to the older person, their family and friends.

Who needs a Geriatric Care Manager?

The concept of geriatric care management has been a part of our culture for many years. In today's busy world both spouses are in the workplace, juggling home, work and leisure life. Many of today's baby boomers are becoming seniors with even older aging relatives.

Your great uncle whom you do not see very often ends up in the hospital and you are called to make a decision about his future because you are his closest next of kin. You knew he was getting older but had no idea just how major his health problems were until you met with his doctor who has told him he cannot go home and will have to go into a nursing home...

Now you are faced with finding a place where your great uncle can live and where his care needs will be met. You have never been inside a care facility and don't even know where to look or what to look for. How expensive will it be and what can your great uncle afford it? These are just some of the questions to be answered.

On a visit to your parents who live in another city, you notice your mother is having difficulty remembering things and the house is not as tidy as it once was. You look in the refrigerator to find it almost empty. Your father tells you he is concerned about your mother's forgetfulness.

The term dementia immediately pops into your mind and you find yourself somewhat shaken by the thoughts going around in your head. Why haven't you noticed things before? Why hasn't your father mentioned his concerns to you?

The first thing you notice on a trip to see your father who lives in another location is that the grass needs cutting and the hedge is quite overgrown. Newspapers are piled up inside the door and look like they have never been read. The curtains are drawn and your father is still in his pajamas and it is the middle of the afternoon.

Why does the house look so run down? What can possibly be going on in your father's mind? What does he do all day?

These are a few of the situations where a geriatric care manager can step in and help. A geriatric care manager is a professional specializing in helping older people and their families make the right decisions about senior care needs.

Most seniors want to remain at home as long as possible. A geriatric care manager can help find the right resources to enable that to take place. Bringing in the right person to assist with bathing, grooming, dressing and eating can make a big difference in the senior's life. Arranging for the proper equipment such as grab bars for the bath, raised toilet seats, canes or walkers will allow the senior to remain independent longer. Perhaps they can go to a senior center or to an adult day program for those with a dementia. Maybe the older person is depressed and with a trip to the family doctor can receive medication to bring them out of that depression. Perhaps a referral to the right medical specialist who can suggest a change in the medication regime will make a difference to the lethargy an older person is demonstrating.

A geriatric care manager knows and understands what resources are best needed to assist the senior. They have training in nursing, social work, gerontology and counseling and have extensive knowledge of the availability and quality of services and of their costs in the senior's community.

Government services for seniors are stretched to the limit, making it necessary for families to seek private resources. Geriatric care managers can mix and match services so that all the senior's needs are met.

When a move to a care facility is required, a geriatric care manager can point out the best ones to meet the senior's individual medical, social and financial requirements. Educating the family and senior about age related changes are other ways of offering support in caring for a senior. Whatever your senior care concerns are, a geriatric care manager is the best source to turn to in time of need.

Like other professionals, geriatric care managers work on a fee for service basis. Typically an initial report is prepared to outline the goals of the family, the obstacles and concerns, and the most effective way of achieving the family's goals commensurate with the family's values. Once a plan has been formulated the geriatric care manager can help the family and senior carry it out. For busy families or for adult children who live in another location, a geriatric care manager will monitor the senior making changes as needed and keeping in regular contact with the family.

10
Coping with Dementia

"I can't find my keys." "You must be getting Alzheimer's," a friend or relative might jokingly reply. Inability to recall the name of a person or place can evoke the same response. As people age, their cognitive abilities generally remain intact, but there's a slowing down of processes, and moments of forgetfulness occur more frequently. However, if they become habitual and begin to interfere with normal life, they could be symptoms of dementia.

The dementia commonly seen in old age used to be called senility. The term is applied to a progressive, degenerative neurological condition that attacks the brain, resulting in memory loss, and an inability to perform familiar tasks. It can also affect personality, language use, and behavior.

Alzheimer's disease is one form of dementia. Other forms include Lewy Bodies disease, Parkinson's disease, picks disease, and multiple infarct dementia, which is caused by strokes.

Dementia usually strikes adults only in their late 70s and 80s; more rarely, it can appear as early as the 30s. There's no effective treatment for dementia. While some medications slow its progression, none has proven effective long term.

Causes and Development

As explained earlier, the ongoing study of 678 elderly nuns at the Sisters of Notre Dame School, in Mankato, Minnesota, has used information obtained before the onset of dementia to explore its causes. The convent has kept accurate records about its residents throughout their lives, making it an ideal situation for researchers. As well, all live in the same environment, eating the same food, breathing the same air, getting similar amounts of exercise. As the nuns have died, their brains have been removed and analyzed.

From this study, it's now known that Alzheimer's disease takes several decades to develop and that it affects all aspects of a person's life. Many of the nuns who've lived long lives without mental deterioration, expressed more complex thinking and more positive emotions in autobiographical essays they had written in their 20s.

It's not yet known whether the early brain development determines an individual's general level of mental activity or his or her likelihood of developing Alzheimer's disease, or whether a positive outlook throughout life is a key to longevity and may delay the onset of Alzheimer's disease.

What is known, is that age is the most common risk factor for Alzheimer's disease. As many as half of those who live to 85, will probably develop it. Typically, they'll live from 10 to 20 years after the first diagnosis. The younger an individual is when diagnosed, the fewer his or her remaining years are likely to be.

Diagnosing Dementia

Social skills are often the last vestiges of an individual's former self to go when he or she has dementia. This can make dementia harder to diagnose. Should a family doctor ask an elderly lady her age, she may reply, "A lady never tells her age." If asked to write out a sentence, a senior may reply, "I've misplaced my glasses."

The earliest signs of impending dementia may be memory loss and impaired judgement. At this stage, symptoms can be quite easy to cover up, and changes are not as likely to be acknowledged by family members and friends. They may be mistakenly attributed to stress or depression.

It's only when you become less spontaneous and have less "sparkle" that people begin to wonder whether these changes are indeed signs of dementia. Eventually, you may have difficulty finding the right words and be much less discriminating in your behavior.

Your reactions will slow along with your ability to learn new things. Often, you'll become angry for no apparent reason. You'll begin to shy away from unfamiliar things, preferring the familiar. Despite these changes, you're still able to accomplish most of the tasks of daily living. Even though you've always behaved with dignity, you may suddenly begin to behave inappropriately.

The manager of the condominium where Edwin's father lived, called to tell him his father had been found wandering the halls at night, knocking on doors and disturbing his neighbors. Since Edwin had infrequent contact with his father, he was so shocked by this call, he didn't even know where to begin.

Tests focusing on cognitive ability, coupled with a medical examination, and perhaps a CAT scan or MRI (which give more informative imaging than X-rays), can help diagnose dementia.

Progressive Changes to Expect

Assistance may be required with mental aspects of related tasks, such as doing simple calculations or balancing a check book. Making simple decisions, even about what clothing to wear or food to eat, may become more difficult. Your speech slows and you're less able to understand what's happening around you. In telling a story, you frequently lose continuity and become frustrated, possibly angry; you may repeat the same story over and over. Insensitivity to the feelings of others is common at this stage. This is usually when the task of care-giving becomes monumental and when bathing, grooming, and even eating become major hurdles.

By the time assistance is needed in all aspects of care, there are usually also significant behavioral changes. Simple tasks need to be repeated many times. Orientation in time and place is lost and you become quite lethargic. You often have no recent memory, but past memories are ever present. You may call your daughter your wife. You may call your brother your father. You no longer show the warmth people normally show toward others. You begin to invent words or use incorrect words. You're uncertain how to act in any situation.

As dementia increases, you become incontinent, have no memory, recent or distant, and have difficulty negotiating even familiar places. You recognize no one.

Living with a spouse or loved one suffering from dementia can be extremely stressful. It can be just as stressful to place that person in a care facility. How do you cope with a relative who suffers from dementia?

Coping Strategies

Communication

Always remember the importance of touch, maintaining eye contact, and being gentle.

• Approach the person slowly to avoid frightening him or her. Sudden movement toward a person with dementia can be perceived as threatening.

• Stand in front of the person and speak his or her name while maintaining eye contact.

• Speak clearly, using short, simple sentences. Present only one topic/question at a time and allow time for the person to respond.

• Always smile when talking to the person, even if he or she is unable to converse with you.

Aggressive Behavior

Activities of daily living such as bathing, grooming, dressing, and eating become strange to a person with dementia. His or her mind may not understand such processes. Try to maintain a sense of humor and not be offended by negative outbursts by someone with dementia. They're not personal.

• Proceed slowly with the task. Continually reassure the person that all is well.

• Don't pull or push the person roughly when they are uncooperative. The person doesn't know they are being unhelpful.

• Try to distract the person by placing something in their hand, a cup, a towel, any object that can't cause harm. Alternatively, you could suggest an activity the person enjoys, such as going for a walk.

• Angry outbursts are often over with quickly and are soon forgotten, providing they're not dwelt on unnecessarily by the caregiver.

Hygiene

As dementia progresses, so does the individual's inability to care for him or herself. However, it's important to let the person with dementia do as much as possible, allowing them to maintain dignity.

• Do not allow the person to bathe or shave alone.

• Check the temperature of the water to make certain it's not too hot or cool.

• Use only a small amount of water in the tub.

• Make certain the person's teeth are brushed.

• Take the person to the toilet (or suggest he or she go on his or her own) at regular intervals.

• If incontinence is a concern, purchase disposable products that are hygienic and allow for dignity. Some products are pad-and-pant systems that can be concealed well under clothing.

Meal Times

A person with dementia should continue to feed him or herself as long as possible, following these suggestions:

• serve only one food type at a time;

• cut food into small pieces to make it easier for the person to handle and to prevent choking. It's preferable to use a spoon only, rather than a knife and fork;

• keep the soup or beverage warm and only half-fill the vessel to avoid spillage.

If the person needs to be fed, follow these instructions:

• sit on the person's dominant side. Bring a spoonful of food slowly within eye range and touch the person's mouth gently until it opens;

• if the person shows signs of restlessness, try holding his or her hand to make him or her feel secure;

• keep the presentation of food simple. Don't clutter the area with sugar, salt, or pepper; a person with dementia may try to put the containers in his or her mouth because they don't recognize them for what they are;

• if coughing or chocking occurs repeatedly during feeding, **seek medical attention as soon as possible.**

If a loved one is in an institutional setting, it's helpful to coincide visits with meals so your help is readily available if needed.

Wandering

Often, people with dementia wander outside and get lost, without being appropriately attired.

• Place bolts and safety locks on all doors to ensure the person can't get out on their own.

• Label clothing and have the person wear an identification bracelet such as those supplied by Medic Alert.

• Take the person for walks in the neighborhood and make certain you announce to them, when you return, "We're home," as a person with dementia can confuse what "home" means. This also creates an opportunity for neighbors to become aware of the situation and recognize the person with dementia should they wander.

• If the person goes missing, try not to panic; sometimes a person with dementia can find their own way back. Begin a neighborhood search immediately and alert the local police right away.

Night-time Concerns

Inability to sleep and wandering make nighttime the most difficult time for caregivers.

• Keep the person physically active as much as possible during the day, so they will be ready to rest at night. If the person naps during the day, keep the nap short (less than an hour).

• Again, make certain the outside doors are securely closed and locked.

• Make use of nightlights in the hall and bathroom.

Try to get some sleep when the person you're caring for sleeps, so you can maintain your own energy level.

Safety Measures

• Do not leave a confused or disoriented individual at home alone.

• Install safety bars in the tub area and around the toilet for easy usage.

• Turn down the temperature control on the hot water heater so the person can't scald him or herself.

• Do not allow the person to use the stove or other appliances, or to bath or shave, without supervision.

• Have safety locks installed on all outer doors.

• Remove the bathroom lock.

• If the person is a smoker, never leave them alone to smoke.

• For driving issues, see the section on driving in chapter 9.

Legal Matters

• Try to get the person to set up Powers of Attorney, for both personal care and finances, before they become mentally incompetent.

• Have the person's doctor assess the person's ability to make decisions for him or herself.

• Consult a lawyer to draw up the necessary legal papers assigning someone to be responsible for their affairs (see chapter 6).

Activities for Seniors with Dementia

Music and Dance

Every day is filled with sound—horns blaring, dogs barking, children playing. Many people listen to CDs or a favorite radio station while driving to work, as well as in their leisure time. They choose to attend the symphony, the opera, or a rock concert because the music is entertaining or inspiring to them.

Music is a great way to communicate with a person with dementia. He or she will respond in different ways, depending on the type of music played; reminders of both good times and bad are found in music. For a person with dementia, hearing an old song from his or her youth, can spark a whole string of memories. Care facilities employing music therapists have been astounded by the benefit to the residents.

Julie has fairly advanced Alzheimer's. Her favorite time of the week is Wednesday at 10:00 a.m., when it's rhythm band practice. The residents prepare for many events within the home, and when they perform, they're greeted with great enthusiasm. Even those, like Julie, who've lost many of their abilities, are able to shake a tambourine or hit a triangle. Just being part of the band gives them a sense of accomplishment. The bandleader is a saxophonist who plays all the old songs, encouraging participation from the band and listeners, who often hum along.

Offer a person with dementia the opportunity of getting up and dancing to music. Ballroom dancing is an activity that can be performed easily if one spouse or partner has dementia but the other does not. This activity is something they can both enjoy. Folk dancing doesn't require a partner, and following simple steps, or just moving to the music, can give a person with dementia a wonderful sense of well-being.

Photographs

Putting together a family photo album is an activity for everyone. A person with dementia is able to draw on long-term memory when shown photos of his or her childhood and early parenting years. They may not always remember everything, but with prompting and assistance from family members, it's surprising what stories will come from viewing photographs. If you work together with the person with dementia in creating an album, it can give them hours of contentment. When staff members in facilities look at photo albums with the residents, they can gain new insights into that person.

> Kirin put together a reminiscing area in his mother's room, giving his mother permission to go back in time, but within the context of today.

People with dementia frequently live in the past, and family members and friends may fail to recognize that's where they're most comfortable. If possible, help the person with dementia bring their past into the present.

Walking

One of the best forms of exercise and activity for a person with dementia is walking. It's something people with dementia are prone to do on their own anyway; this is frequently termed "wandering," especially if there's no purpose to it. However, walks in the neighborhood, to the store, or in the country are excellent outlets for a senior whether he or she is cognitively impaired or not. Most care facilities don't have enough staff to supervise this activity, so it's not encouraged. However, those at home can go out with a friend, family member, or caregiver. Walking can provide hours of entertainment, and a chance to birdwatch, window-shop or purchase groceries, or other items.

Reading

Despite his or her inability to remember recent events, a person with dementia can find being read to soothing and relaxing. The need for quiet time is just as important to a person being cared for, as to a caregiver, and time shared this way is valuable to both participants. Read news stories from the local and national newspapers, a short story from a magazine, or an excerpt from a novel. If you choose to read a longer story, each time you get together, review what's already been read.

Give your relative lots of hugs. Assist your loved one in maintaining his or her dignity as he or she passes through the various stages of dementia. It can be extraordinarily painful to watch someone you love fade away, and heartbreaking to no longer be recognized by them. As the person with dementia retreats farther into the past, try your best to live in and appreciate the present. This is true at all times, but particularly when coping with the slow loss of a loved one to dementia.

Part III

Financial Planning

11

Why Plan?

Today's financial decisions determine tomorrow's financial destiny. This is true at all stages of life.

A young man in his 20s received a raise and decided to spend the extra $250 a month for a slightly nicer apartment and a few more evenings out. If directed to his Individual Retirement Account ("IRA"), over the next 30 years, with a 7.0% return, this $250 per month would accumulate to almost $305,000.

A couple in their 40s decide to use investment assets to upgrade from a $250,000 to a $400,000 home. The increased costs of the larger home mean they can save less; meanwhile, they've converted $150,000 of their invested assets into personal assets. At an average return of 7.0%, 20 years later, the net result of their decision is approximately $581,000 less in invested assets. The cost of moving from a $250,000 to a $400,000 home is significant and the financial impact it will have on this couple's accumulated assets at retirement is very meaningful.

A couple in their late 60s has accumulated considerable wealth and live well off the interest income from their $2 million portfolio. However, they do no tax or investment planning. Twenty years later, their beneficiaries receive $2 million. Simple estate and tax-planning strategies could have easily doubled this amount.

All the parts of your financial world are interconnected. Each time you make a purchase, choose an investment, or borrow money without fully analyzing the options and long-term impact—whenever you make financial decisions in isolation—you reduce your chances of meeting your goals. Financial security and prosperity usually result from making many small choices, through the years, rather than from a few big decisions.

To manage your money and assets effectively, you need to make decisions on a strategic basis. The best way to do this is by working with a qualified financial advisor.

Objectives of Financial Planning

Financial independence is when you have the time and money, to celebrate independence every day...freedom from work...freedom from want...freedom from worry.

• Set and actively pursue your financial goals: Planning encourages you to decide what you want to achieve, and when: in the short-term (the next 2 years), in an intermediate time frame (2 to 10 years), and in the long-term. Building a financial plan helps you judge what goals are attainable, ascertain the trade-offs that may be necessary, and find actions that will help you achieve your goals. Having a plan of action to reach your goals strongly enhances your chances of success. You may find yourself able to dream bigger dreams.

• Live well: Whatever lifestyle you desire, financial planning will help you achieve it. The level of expense that represents your ideal lifestyle, whether it's high or low, will have a large impact on your financial plan. Consumption is high on some people's lists. Others concentrate on accumulating wealth. Most try to balance the two.

• Spend wisely: Financial planning encourages a systematic approach to spending. It helps you consider the best timing and the strengths and weaknesses of each decision. It helps you allocate amounts for expenses and amounts for acquiring assets to help you achieve your goals. Having clearly defined goals helps you avoid impulse purchases and risky investments.

• Avoid needless expenses: Do you want to pay more in taxes, interest charges, and other financial fees and penalties than you need to? Of course not. But if you don't have a well-thought-out financial plan, it's likely, you're doing just that.

• Protect yourself and your assets: Sudden death, disability, extended unemployment, prolonged sickness, the requirement of homecare, time spent in a long-term care facility—financial stress, that could've been avoided, compounds the difficulties of such situations. Anticipating potential crises, examining your financial options ahead of time, and making decisions in advance can eliminate many costly mistakes. For most, having insurance coverage is crucial, but having too much or too little can be inefficient or self-destructive. A good financial plan will help you devise the appropriate insurance portfolio for your situation.

• Know where you stand: Developing a financial plan provides peace of mind; you have a clear picture of your current financial status, and you know where your plan is flexible if change is needed.

• Focus on what matters: One aspect of your life that can be delegated largely to someone else, is the development of your plan to reach your financial life goals. By delegating this task to a trusted financial advisor, you can focus on the things that matter most to you; family and friends, work and education, community involvement, health, and recreation. Your plan will help make the most of your resources, and realize your aspirations more fully.

• Be prepared: Improved disease treatment and better health in general, have led to longer life spans; at the same time, the costs of medical services have increased, and a growing number of seniors are finding they can no longer manage on their own incomes. Today's adult children, together with older parents, relatives and other family members, need to plan seriously—and at an earlier stage—for the possible financial responsibility of caring for others, and to ensure that there'll be sufficient resources left to care for themselves.

Susan is 50 years old, recently divorced, and has two children attending university. She works full time, but with the cost of providing monthly help to her children, she lives paycheck to paycheck. Marilynn, Susan's mother, has just turned 77, and also requires Susan's financial help on a regular basis. Marilynn's government support (Social Security) along with her limited investment assets, don't always cover the monthly expenses of health care and living in her own home. Susan spends a couple of nights a week, and most of her weekends, traveling to her mother's home to help with household chores. She often finds herself worrying about her financial future, and is concerned that she may one day have to depend on her own children.

Hans and Annika are in their early 50s and plan to retire in five years. Both have incomes that place them in the highest marginal tax bracket. Both have been able to save a good portion of their monthly income while maintaining a comfortable lifestyle. Both feel they've done a good job of preparing for their future, and currently, don't see any shortfalls. Hans's parents are both in reasonably good health and seem able to sustain a fairly comfortable lifestyle. Hans is somewhat concerned, however, because he's not sure of their financial position. He's never approached the subject of finances with his parents because he doesn't want to embarrass them or suggest they needed his help. Annika's parents, on the other hand, joke about how they always face a negative cash flow when the end of the month rolls around. Annika's dad has an illness that limits his activity and requires constant medical attention. Annika has offered financial help to her parents, but they've refused it, saying they don't want to be a burden to their daughter's family.

Why People Don't Plan Financially

"When I begin my new career, I'll be ready to plan for the future." "When I get my raise, I'll have enough to finally start preparing a financial plan." "When I have more time to plan, I know I will." "I have enough resources to last, and I'll prepare my plan when I retire." "We don't need to plan. We're retired, live on a fixed income, and are doing okay." Many of us fall victim to making promises to ourselves but never fulfill those promises. We assure ourselves that we'll get serious about preparing for our financial future at some unspecified time.

Perhaps you feel unprepared for the commitments you may have to make to reach your goals. A financial plan may require you to make changes or sacrifices in your current habits or lifestyle. But if you wait, you may have to make even bigger sacrifices. You might have to work for 10 years longer. You might have to reduce your lifestyle habits considerably to avoid running out of capital, wealth or property you can use to produce more income or wealth. You might even have to depend on your children to support you in your old age.

Often, people feel overwhelmed by the concept of preparing a financial plan and intimidated by the apparent size and complexity of the task. Because they don't know how to plan financially, they resort to no planning at all. They may be unaware of the many tools available to assist with personal financial planning, or of how to find an experienced and knowledgeable financial advisor to work with them in developing their financial plan. Instead, they find themselves making financial decisions on an as-needed basis.

Some who are well aware of the benefits of financial planning, still don't have a plan. Here are some common misperceptions about financial planning.

MYTH **Financial planning is only for those with lots of money.** Do you think you need a significant income, or at least a million in investment assets, to justify having a financial plan? People with less money benefit from planning even more than those who're wealthy, simply because their need to make the most of each dollar is greater.

Do you currently live paycheck to paycheck, thinking that when you make more money, planning will become an option? It's more likely that, as your income grows, so will your lifestyle costs. There are those who say their annual income of $35,000 is inadequate to cover monthly expenses, and those who say $100,000 a year won't cover their lifestyle needs. No matter what your income, financial planning can be a challenge. Often, the greater the challenges you face, the more you have to gain from a personally structured, long-term plan.

Do you think those with higher incomes have different, better opportunities to build wealth? Actually, although the benefits to someone with a lower income may be smaller in size, planning benefits individuals in all income brackets in similar ways. Successful management of your income, no matter what size, increases the likelihood you'll achieve your goals.

MYTH **Preparing a financial plan is too expensive.**
Do you think hiring a financial advisor would cost more than you can afford? In fact, the real costs of not planning, such as unnecessary taxes, interest costs, and risk exposure, or costs resulting from inefficient asset allocation and estate strategies, usually far outweigh the cost of developing a financial plan. A financial advisor will help you budget for the expense, and some of the strategies your advisor develops for you, such as increasing annual tax deductions or deferrals to increase current cash flow, can even pay for initial fees.

Much, if not all, of the cost of planning may be built into the cost of the financial products or services you already use. Some financial advisors deduct from their annual planning fee the amount they expect to receive annually in commissions. If your investment assets are substantial, the entire upfront cost of your financial plan may even be offset by the compensation your advisor receives from managing your investment portfolio.

MYTH **Planning will take too much time and effort.**
A person who plans actually spends less time on financial matters than someone who does no planning at all. People with no plan often find themselves lurching from one financial crisis to another. Financial planning doesn't eliminate surprises or adverse developments, but it lets you deal with them better because you know your options, so managing your personal affairs becomes less stressful.

MYTH **Revealing the state of my financial affairs will be too embarrassing.**

People who have planned well financially all their lives, without professional help, are extremely rare. Be assured that there are many people whose affairs are in far worse shape than yours. Like a doctor or lawyer, a qualified financial advisor will help you solve problems constructively, supportively, and ethically.

MYTH **Once you're past a certain age, it's too late to plan.**

Some people think that by 65 or 70, planning is no longer effective. While it's too late to plan for past events, it's never too late to plan for the future. Maximizing your current retirement income, reducing taxes payable, ensuring you'll have adequate healthcare and long-term care if needed, and designing an effective estate plan to reduce costs and ensure your wishes are carried out, are only a few of the relevant concerns in your retirement years. A financial plan will help determine whether or not your resources are sufficient to provide for your current lifestyle, if you need to reduce your lifestyle costs or could even increase your lifestyle costs. At all stages of life, financial planning has the same goal: enjoyment of life and peace of mind, knowing you'll be okay and that things will be looked after. Financial planning is beneficial to anyone, regardless of age or circumstances.

12

Your Financial Plan

You've only so much money, but so many ways you could use it. Different choices will lead, ultimately, to different outcomes. How do you decide? You know your immediate needs, and that you must balance your expenses and income. But what about reducing and deferring current and future taxes, accumulating savings to meet future goals, providing for your current or future retirement, and protecting yourself against possible risks? Not to forget designing an estate plan for the effective management and disposition of your assets at a minimal cost. To ensure that you can meet your financial needs now and in the future, you need a plan.

Financial planning is the process of examining your current financial resources, defining realistic short- and long-term financial goals, and developing and implementing strategies for reaching those goals.

Isaiah and Deb, in their late 30s, seemed never to have enough income to meet their needs, let alone save for the future. They decided they needed help in putting their financial affairs in order. They met with a financial advisor to discuss their situation. After developing a financial plan, they realized that their current lifestyle expenditures were far more than they had thought. Their advisor had drawn up an annual cash-flow statement detailing their expenses. It revealed areas where they could actually reduce costs and create more on the bottom line for saving toward their goals without making any painful sacrifices. In addition, their advisor developed tax strategies that reduced current taxation and further increased their cash-flow surplus.

Principles of Financial Planning

• **Everyone should have a plan to become, and remain, financially independent; to accumulate sufficient resources to meet all his or her future income requirements.**

Your financial plan should be a written, comprehensive plan outlining your goals and objectives. Goals are what you hope to achieve. Objectives quantify the goals and make them specific. For example:

Goal: Retire early.
Objective: Retire at age 61 on an annual net-after-tax income of $42,000 indexed to inflation.

Goal: Leave as much as we can to our children, but live comfortably for as long as we're alive.
Objective: Maintain an annual net-after-tax income to meet our needs of $52,000 indexed to inflation. Be able to spend up to an additional $10,000–$15,000 a year on

travel. Maintain a substantial safety net to cover emergencies. Leave our children $100,000 each and provide $20,000 for each grandchild's education.

Having a written plan creates a "track to run on," helps you avoid costly mistakes, and provides a much greater assurance of getting what you want out of life.

• **The plan should be shared with all mature family members.**
You have your own, individual priorities. Family members may have different priorities. It's important to have the consensus of family members on key goals.

• **Appreciable wealth isn't created overnight; it requires time.**
Think of wealth as the amount of money required to sustain your lifestyle for the rest of your life. The sooner you begin, the more easily creation of meaningful wealth can be accomplished. "Procrastination is the thief of time," wrote poet Edward Young. The best time to begin planning is today.

• **Once created, personal wealth should be preserved.**
Money's hard to get, but easy to lose. Attention should always be given to the preservation of wealth through the creation of an estate plan. A properly conceived estate plan will help to mitigate the destruction of wealth caused by death, disability, or even financial disaster.

• **Today's decisions will determine tomorrow's financial destiny.**
Your current circumstances are the result of decisions made in the past. By being proactive, you increase the likelihood of meeting your needs and desires in the future, and reduce the roadblocks that may be encountered along the way.

• **No final decisions should be made without first considering all the facts.**

Because the decisions you make today will determine your future security and prosperity, it's vital to establish a framework for making well-founded, strategic decisions.

• **Few people are able to be totally objective about their own personal situation.**

This is why professional athletes have coaches, and doctors don't treat themselves or close family members. Similarly, most people do better financially when they use a trusted, suitably qualified financial advisor.

• **Attainment of your goals and objectives should be a shared responsibility with a financial advisor.**

The goals and objectives are yours. The advice is the financial advisor's, but the decision to act on it is yours as well. Thus reaching your goals and objectives is indeed a shared responsibility with your advisor.

The Role of a Financial Advisor

Whether a personal trainer, doctor, accountant, or lawyer, few people are authorities on more than one subject or in more than one profession. Even those who are multitalented will concede that they're a specialist in one area or another. Should you seek advice regarding a personal fitness program, or a medical, legal, or financial concern, your best solution is always to look for a specialist in that particular field. A financial advisor is someone who specializes in the fields of personal finance and investment management. He or she may also have knowledge and experience in various other fields, such as tax, estate planning, or risk management.

A common misconception is that financial planning refers to investment advice alone. Your financial plan should reflect not only up-to-date investment and economic information, but also current tax, estate, and retirement developments. All these components are linked, and a decision in one affects the others. For example, a decision regarding investments will have an impact on current and future taxation, or a retirement goal will have an effect on your estate. Knowledge of these various components is vital to the success of your plan. When they're integrated successfully, your financial plan is much more effective.

Few individuals have the considerable time and expertise for researching, implementing, and monitoring a financial plan, or the inclination. Even if you do have the expertise, you may not be willing to devote the necessary time to staying informed on economic changes, investment fluctuations and opportunities, and tax and estate legislation. Some individuals do their own financial planning and do it well, but for most, a financial advisor is an invaluable partner in reaching their financial goals. Chapter 17 offers guidance on selecting a financial advisor.

Good decisions result from good decision-making mechanisms. Unfortunately, financial decisions are often based on an emotion of the moment, an approaching deadline, a friend's opinion, or unfounded fears caused by lack of knowledge, or they're made in haste, after a crisis.

Whether you decide to create your own financial plan, or work with a financial advisor, you should follow an orderly thought process that's methodical and comprehensive.

Steps in Financial Planning

A financial plan involves six basic steps. Three of these steps always rest with you:

- stating your goals and objectives;
- providing complete information regarding your financial affairs;
- deciding to act on recommendations.

The other three steps of the decision-making process are the responsibility of a financial advisor:

- conducting the analysis;
- designing the strategy;
- providing advice to make the strategy work.

1. Goals and Objectives

First, decide what you want to accomplish. Setting goals will give you a sense of purpose and provide a sound basis for future financial decisions. Goals provide reference points to measure your progress and show you what actions are needed. To develop your financial goals and objectives:

- decide what you want to do;
- decide when you want to do it;
- estimate the costs of each objective;
- analyze whether you can attain those goals.

For example, if you decide to retire, ask yourself:

- When would I like to retire?
- How much monthly income will I need to support my chosen lifestyle?
- What else might I need money for (children's education, paying off debts, buying a recreational property, providing assistance to elderly parents, etc.) and when will I need the money?
- What assets will I need to provide this income? How might I create and build these assets?

Your financial goals and objectives will be influenced by the standard of living you wish to maintain, or achieve, and by the extent to which you're prepared to save for the future. Your goals should be as precise as possible. Furthermore, to be meaningful, they should be realistic. The more clearly you define your goals, the more easily you can make decisions that move you toward their attainment.

Anton and Josie were astonished when they met with their financial advisor. Unbeknownst to them, they had completely different goals and objectives. Josie wanted to see her many years of hard work translated into annual vacations and an enriched retirement lifestyle. Priorities for Anton were increased volunteer work for charities and coaching his grandson's hockey team. Anton also wanted to help provide for their grandson's university education and preserve their estate value to pass on to their own children. Working with their advisor on their financial plan, they discovered that with a little compromise on both their parts, they'd be able to fulfill all their goals.

2. Information

Before you can develop a plan to achieve your goals and objectives, you need a clear picture of what you have to work with. Often people make unwise decisions because they fail to fully consider their current position. Your financial plan will only be as good as the data and assumptions you use to formulate it.

The amount of information you need to collect depends on the complexity of your financial situation. The main types of information required are:

• Cash outflow: All money you currently pay to meet your lifestyle expenditures and debt obligations (such as rent or mortgage payments, property taxes, maintenance costs, utilities, services, food costs, household goods, transportation, clothing, daycare, medical and dental expenses, insurance, loan payments, private educational fees, discretionary spending such as entertainment, gifts, holidays, vacations, memberships and charitable contributions, and so on).

• Income and expected future income: Employment income (any money you receive periodically in return for your services), investment income, and pension income.

• Assets: Property (both real estate and personal), financial investments (such as cash, stocks, bonds, or mutual funds), business assets, and any other financial resources you may have.

• Liabilities: All financial obligations and debts (such as mortgages, car loans, personal loans, credit card balances, and deferred income taxes).

• Contingent Liabilities: Costs involved in helping aging parents, or assistance that may be required to help adult children.

• Employment benefits: Both group insurance and pension benefits.

• Insurance: All existing, personally-owned insurance policies (life, disability, long-term care, critical illness, auto, property, and casualty).

• Legal: Summarize existing wills, trusts, Powers of Attorney, marriage contracts, separation agreements, business agreements, and other contractual obligations.

A financial advisor will also want to survey your attitudes toward various types of investments to create a profile of your risk sensitivity.

3. Analysis

Knowing where you want to go (goals and objectives) and where you are now (information) enables you or your financial advisor to decide what types of analysis are required. Analysis should answer questions about your current situation such as: Are you heading in the right direction to achieve your goals and objectives? Where might there be problems and opportunities? What are specific areas of vulnerability? Basic components of this analysis are:

• a detailed statement of net worth, including all personal and invested assets, as well as all liabilities based on the most recent values available;

• a personal cash-flow projection of all expected revenue and expenses for the next 12 months;

• an income-tax projection for the current calendar year, considering extraordinary tax events specific to your situation, as well as basic tax exemptions.

How will your surviving family members be financially positioned in the event of your death, or that of a spouse or partner? What will be the financial impact on your family if you're disabled? To answer these questions, and to be able to take action to solve identified problems, you'll need:

• an analysis of your situation in the event of premature death or disability.

The analysis may also include:

• an examination of your existing investments;

• an analysis of the projected settlement costs of your estate at the time of death.

Of all financial objectives, that of attaining financial independence is pivotal. Thus, you will also need:

• an analysis to identify if you have, or are accumulating, sufficient resources to meet all your future income requirements.

Only after completing the appropriate analyses of your current situation, will you be in a position to develop a meaningful personal financial strategy.

4. Financial Strategy

To attempt to reach your goals, without a written strategy, would be like trying to build a home without an architectural plan. Fundamental strategic elements include:

• a calculation of how much you need to save each year, or how much you're able to spend each year if you're already retired;

• a plan for how your debt will be reduced over time;

• the target rate of return on your investments, taking into account your sensitivity to investment risk.

A financial strategy is actually a set of instructions, or a prescription, for what changes need to occur in your current behavior. It can be likened to going to your doctor for a check-up; your doctor might tell you to make some changes in your diet, to exercise more, or perhaps to have additional tests to ensure optimal healthcare. Similarly, a financial strategy will tell you if you have to change your saving or spending patterns, or if you should adjust your approach to investment decisions. It might also tell you that it's impossible for you to achieve all of your financial objectives, given your current resources. This will mean either revising your expectations, or devising a viable way to increase your earnings. The key is to have a sound strategy upon which your future financial decisions can be based.

The principles of personal cash and tax management are discussed in detail in the next chapter. Chapters 14, 15, and 16 are devoted to investment management, risk management, and estate management, respectively. Each of these areas should be covered in your financial plan.

5. Action Plan

Your action plan (financial advisors often call this "Advice and Recommendations") should provide a specific outline of the steps you need to take to make your financial strategy work.

Anna's strategy involved saving $10,000 each year to meet her future lifestyle requirements. Her current cash flow indicated that she could save only $5,000. The advice given by her financial advisor included specific ideas for reducing expenses, such as lowering her taxes, and reducing the carrying cost of her debt, to make it possible to save the full $10,000.

The target rate of return of Victor's investments was 7%. He was currently only averaging 5%. His financial advisor

Your Financial Plan 179

detailed what changes he needed to make in his asset allocation to average a 7% return on a long-term basis.

Advice and recommendations should also be developed to make certain that other, non-accumulation objectives, such as the distribution of your estate at time of death, are achieved. If you're already financially independent, your action plan will focus predominantly on non-accumulation objectives.

6. Decisions for Action

A plan is only a plan until it's put into action. To turn your objectives into reality, you must follow the strategy and advice. You may choose to implement your plan in stages, depending on your current financial situation. However, it's essential that you do carry out your plan in order to gain benefit from the planning process.

The decisions for action are your responsibility, but a good financial advisor will make it easier, by continuing to work with you, offering gentle nudges as required. Be sure to keep your advisor informed of changes in your personal situation, such as pay increases or decreases, employment benefits, legacies, lifestyle expenditures, and responsibilities or personal family situations.

Bill worked for the same company for 30 years. He'd just retired. His retirement benefits included a sizable annual pension. Bill and his wife, Maria, were both in their early 50s. They were looking forward to having more time for travel, social clubs, and hobbies—and for their teenage son, who was still living at home. Bill and Maria were delighted when they received their financial plan from their advisor. They learned that they'd be able to do a lot more than they'd thought and still leave a sizable inheritance to their son. This was important to them, because they had received inheritances from their own parents that had enabled them to get ahead early in life.

Their financial plan indicated set amounts for their retirement lifestyle, annual vacations, and so on. After their first year of retirement, Bill and Maria sat down with their advisor to review their plan for the following year. They were shocked to discover they'd spent almost $50,000 more on living costs than the amount targeted. A new analysis showed that if they maintained this increased retirement lifestyle cost, they'd run out of money, leaving nothing for their son. After further discussion of their goals, and the collection and analysis of additional information, their advisor was able to revise their plan to allow them to enjoy an increased retirement lifestyle for a set period, and still leave something to their son.

Review and Update

As you go through life, your personal outlook, needs, and financial objectives change, and your financial plan should evolve to reflect those changes.

Review your plan on an annual basis to ensure that it's proceeding according to your expectations, and is still in your best interest. Rarely can a financial plan be developed, set in motion, and then forgotten. You might need to revise your plan due to market fluctuations, new tax legislation, improved and new financial products and services, or a change in your circumstances. Or, the original plan may now be either too conservative or too aggressive. Always remember, your financial plan is flexible and can be modified over time to meet your changing needs and abilities.

Adherence to these six steps will help you achieve your financial objectives more effectively than any other method. Conversely, failure to make decisions strategically often results in years of hardship and disappointment.

When should you start making decisions on a strategic basis? When you're out of debt? When you get organized? The answer is today. Today is the best time to begin. But, don't forget that the process needs to be continuous. Each time objectives are realized, or changed, each time information changes, a new analysis, new strategy, or new advice may be required.

> Roger and Luisa, both in their early 60s, were meeting with Don, their investment advisor, to discuss their upcoming fixed-income product maturities. Don learned that Roger and Luisa had other small investments elsewhere, that weren't performing well and that they feared their investments would prove inadequate to last them the remainder of their lives. Don suggested they speak with one of the financial advisors at his firm to determine if there were ways they could improve their situation. The couple was doubtful much could be done so late in life, but Don was persistent. He convinced them that, if nothing else, it would be better to know where they stood, than continue in stressful uncertainty. After reviewing their affairs with a financial advisor, Roger and Luisa found that changes could be made to their current situation that would enable them to have sufficient retirement income. The peace of mind they gained was overwhelming, and they thank Don every time they meet with their financial advisor.

How long should you continue to make decisions on a strategic basis? Until you're financially independent? Until you're on track? The answer is, quite simply, always. Following this process allows you to create and preserve wealth, sparing yourself much hardship and enabling you to enjoy a future far more comfortable than you might have imagined possible. Begin making all your financial decisions on a strategic basis now.

If today's decisions determine tomorrow's financial destiny, shouldn't today's decisions always be the right ones?

13

Boosting the Bottom Line

Cash management. Sounds dull, doesn't it? But whether you're 40, 60, or 80, properly managing your cash is the key to maximizing your financial resources, which sounds rather appealing. Cash management is the process of controlling expenses, minimizing taxes, and reducing the cost of debt to maximize the bottom line.

During your working years, your main source of revenue is your employment income. If the cash coming in doesn't exceed what's going out to cover basic living expenses, there'll be nothing left for savings. But if—as you should—you aim to be financially independent some day, some of what you earn needs to be saved, to build enough capital to support future expenditures. Managing your cash flow well will help you save.

If you're retired, your sources of revenue will be pension income, government benefits, and investment income. If this revenue doesn't meet your living expenses, you'll have to draw more income from your assets; if it exceeds them, you will have a surplus that can be reinvested. Likely, you saved in the past to support your current lifestyle. Now, cash management will help you use your revenues efficiently to meet your retirement needs.

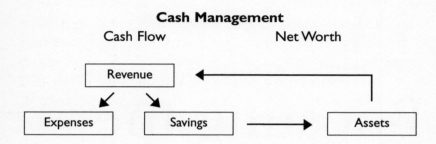

Cash Management

Cash Flow   Net Worth

New wealth is only created by saving. And to save, you need to manage your cash-flow effectively.

Beginning when she was 35 years old, Edna contributed $2,000 a year to an IRA for 8 successive years, and stopped contributing in year 9. Managing her IRA through the years, she averaged a return of 7.0%. By the time she reached age 65, she had $90,910 in her IRA.

Noah began his IRA contributions of $2,000 per year at age 44. He invested his $2,000 the same way Edna had and continued to do so for the next 21 years. Noah averaged the same return of 7.0% and, when he was 65, his investment was worth $89,730. He had invested for 13 more years than Edna, but had $1,180 less.

Principles of Cash Management

• Pay yourself first
There are always too many things you could spend money on. This is true whether you earn $50,000 or $500,000 a year. In fact, those who earn $500,000 a year often have as much, or more,

difficulty saving than those who earn $50,000. Most people save only what's left, after everything else is paid.

How do you save first, and then spend? The solution is not usually a budget. Like diets, budgets seldom work over the long-term. To lose weight and keep it off, you need to change your lifestyle, by changing your eating habits. Similarly, to save effectively, you need to make saving a natural part of your cash management practices. The best way to do this is to set up an automatic savings plan, whereby you arrange for a specified amount to be deducted automatically from your personal bank account (weekly, bi-weekly, monthly, or even quarterly) and invested in the vehicle of your choice. Once this is established, saving requires virtually no time or effort.

What amount should you pay yourself? For some, 10% will be more than enough to enable them to reach their financial objectives; for others who're starting later, it may take 25%. It all depends on how far you have to go to arrive at your financial destination, and how much time you have to get there. This is why having a personal savings strategy is important.

> René had always known he needed to save to meet his goal of retiring at age 65. He was now 38, however, and so far hadn't managed to save anything. There always seemed to be something else he needed instead. René decided it was time to get serious. He met with a financial advisor to determine what he needed to do meet his retirement goal.
>
> After reviewing the plan developed for him, René was amazed to find that his plan provided not only an investment strategy; it also provided cash-management solutions and tax and risk-management strategies. He discovered various areas where he needed to make changes but, most importantly, the plan demonstrated how much he needed to save to reach his goal. To help

René save, his advisor set up a regular monthly withdrawal from René's personal bank account that would automatically be invested according to his investment-management strategy. This was the perfect solution for René. He didn't have to take time from his busy schedule every month to meet with his investment advisor, nor did he have to worry about what amount to save, or how he was going to save. In the end, René realized that saving for his retirement was the real necessity that was lacking in his life.

What if you're already retired, or have achieved financial independence? Then, the answer to how much you should save is probably nothing. It's an activity you engaged in, in the past. Should you fall into this category, you can probably skip the next three principles and proceed to the last, planning to maximize your net after-tax income.

• Do not presume upon tomorrow

You need to ensure that your income, and your ability to maintain your family's lifestyle, won't be interrupted by premature death or disability. Devoting a small portion of your employment income to acquiring the appropriate insurance can achieve this.

You should also plan to build and maintain an adequate cash reserve for emergency purposes. Three to five months' income is a guideline, but this can vary considerably depending on the volatility of your employment income and individual circumstances.

Last, but not least, you must make sure you don't live beyond your means.

Michael and Nalini hoped to retire when Michael was 55, on an after-tax income of $75,000 per year. They knew from their financial plan that, to achieve their goal, they needed to save $15,000 each year, indexed to inflation, until Michael was 55. They saved that amount without difficulty for several years. Meanwhile, Nalini started earning more and Michael began getting bonuses. They were saving a fixed amount, but they grew accustomed to spending the rest. The cost of their lifestyle grew quickly. When Michael's bonuses were reduced, and Nalini stopped working, they had to discontinue their savings program just to make ends meet.

You cannot count on money being there tomorrow if you don't start planning and saving today. Working with a financial advisor, who can perform regular updates of your savings and investment strategy, will make adhering to this principle much easier.

• Minimize the cost of your chosen lifestyle
Does 10% sound like an impossible amount to save? Imagine getting a 10% cut in your income as the result of a new tax. At first, you'd definitely notice it, but soon you'd find manageable ways to adjust.

There are many ways you can significantly reduce your current expenses by making only minor adjustments to your lifestyle. Take a close look at your spending habits. Something as simple as choosing no-name products over name brands when buying groceries, can translate into annual savings that, over a period of 10, 20, or 30 years, really build up. One $4.00 café latte each workday adds up to over $1,000 a year. Magazine subscriptions cost a fraction of the newsstand price. By buying second-hand items—electronic appliances, books, designer clothes, and sports equipment, for instance—you can often acquire top-of-the-line products, in good condition, for less than a new, inferior product. Traveling off-season, calling long distance at low-rate times, buying in bulk—the list of potential small savings that will quickly add up to large ones goes on and on. It's usually easier than you might think to reduce your lifestyle costs, particularly once you realize how much you have to gain by doing so.

> Rather than buying a new $50,000 car (monthly payments over a five-year period of around $850), Rosemary opted to acquire a similar, two-year-old vehicle for just $35,000 (monthly payments of around $600 over a five-year period). The difference in monthly payments between the new car and the two-year-old vehicle, resulted in a difference of over $3,000 on an annual basis. By investing the additional $3,000 over the next five years into a portfolio, averaging a 7.0% return, her modest lifestyle adjustment translated into a portfolio enhancement of over $48,000 after 20 years.

• **Avoid non-deductible debt**

Mortgage interest is tax deductible, however other interest such as credit card interest is not tax deductible.

If borrowing to acquire personal assets is unavoidable, never allow your debt-to-asset ratio—your debt obligations divided by your assets—to exceed 75%. For example, if you have $500,000 in assets, your debt should never exceed $375,000 (375,000/500,000 = 75%). Aim to keep this ratio much lower. Non-deductible debt should be minimized and avoided whenever possible.

• **Maximize after-tax discretionary income**

Maximizing after-tax discretionary income doesn't mean minimizing tax at any cost.

> George kept his money in a checking account to avoid paying tax on interest income, not realizing that, after paying tax, he would still have 50% of the income that

his $200,000 earned each year. At only 4%, that would be $4,000 a year.

For more information on this subject, see the detailed section below.

You can maximize after-tax discretionary income in four primary ways: deduct, defer, diminish, and divide.

Deduct

Diligently take advantage of all deductions and credits available to you, based on the normal conduct of your personal financial affairs. This doesn't mean creating tax deductions just to get a tax deduction. There must be an absolute net benefit.

Defer

Defer payment of tax whenever possible. This creates opportunities to do something with the tax dollars you've deferred paying, such as leaving the money invested. A popular and effective way to defer taxes is with IRAs.

The Power of Tax Deferral (Table 1)

Investment Option	Before Tax Dollars Invested Each Year Over a Period of 20 Years	Tax Recovery (40% Marginal Tax Rate)	After Tax Investment Cost	Cumulative Value After 20 Years at 7%	Annual Pre Tax Income Provided For a Period of 26 Years (Annual Rate of Return at 7% and a 40% Marginal Tax Rate)	After Tax Value After Cashing Out Investment at a Marginal Tax Rate of 40%
IRA Investment	$10,000	$4,000	$6,000	$409,954	$31,963	$245,973
Non IRA Investment	$6,000	NIL	$6,000	$190,081	$14,820	$190,081

There are two types of IRAs; Traditional and Roth. Both must be funded with earned income. Traditional IRAs save money and lower tax liability (you may be able to deduct your contributions from your current taxes, but you must begin taking required minimum distributions ("RMDs") at age 70; Roth IRAs avoid RMDs, and distributions are tax free and penalty free provided certain requirements are met. Your financial advisor can provide direction as to which IRA is right for you.

Tax deferral means you owe no taxes on earnings until you begin to withdraw. As a not-so-subtle encouragement to hold these investments until retirement, you may incur a 10% penalty tax to the federal government for withdrawals of taxable earnings, before you reach age 59.

A principal advantage of IRAs is clear: Compounding + tax savings can add up significantly over time. Remember the retirement rule of thumb: you will need roughly 80% of your pre-retirement income to live the way you have grown accustomed to.

Here is an illustration for the power of compounding, a hypothetical illustration.

Adam and Thomas
College graduation

After graduating at age 25, smart-thinking Adam began investing the maximum, $3,000 into his IRA every year and his friend, "I'll think about it later" Thomas spent his money otherwise and told his friend he would think about it later. ($3,000 is the 2004 IRA contribution limit, up to age 50.)

Marriage

They both married at age 33. Adam decided his new family needed to use that $3,000 a year elsewhere and stopped his regular investments. However, marriage made Thomas want to plan better for the future, so he opened an IRA and began investing $3,000 a year.

Retirement

Both Adam and Thomas retired at age 65. Adam's total investment was just still just the $24,000 made when he was young. Thomas had continued with his yearly contributions and invested a total of $99,000. With all dividends and capital gains reinvested you may be surprised to learn that Adam comes out ahead of Thomas, even though he invested far less — that is the power of compounding over time. Adam's total value is: $1,640,081 and Thomas' value is $1,467,059. (This is a hypothetical illustration based on an 8% annual rate of return.)

Some individuals don't invest in IRAs because they're afraid their investment will be tied up and they won't be able to withdraw money in the event of an emergency. This isn't true. If withdrawals are made before you reach age 59 your distribution may be exempt from the 10% early withdrawal penalty if the distribution is:

- part of a series of substantially equal periodic payments;
- for qualified medical expenses in excess of 7.5% of your adjusted gross income;
- to cover qualified health-insurance premiums of certain unemployed individuals;
- used to acquire a first-time principal residence (subject to a $10,000 lifetime limit);
- used to pay qualified higher-education expenses for you/spouse/dependent children;
- made on account of an IRS levy

Diminish

Sometimes, merely changing the type of income can diminish tax. Consider the differences in the taxation of interest income, dividends from stock companies, and capital gains shown in Table 2.

Diminishing Tax by Changing the Type of Income (Table 2)

Source of Income	After-Tax Income on $1,000 (based on 2003 tax laws)	
	Medium Tax Bracket	High Tax Bracket
Salary/Pension Income	$540	$470
Interest Income	$540	$470
Dividend Income	$590	$510
Capital Gains	$770	$735

Divide

In the US progressive tax system, those with the most income pay a higher percentage of tax. A common way to reduce taxes, is by dividing income among family members. Splitting income among family members can significantly increase your income on an annual basis.

Two retired families each have an annual income of $120,000. In the first family, income splitting isn't practiced. One spouse has all the income. The result is an after-tax income of approximately $71,000 per year. The second family planned for years to have their retirement incomes relatively equal. The net result is an after-tax income of $82,000 per year.

Although income splitting can be accomplished at any time, it generally takes years of planning to maximize the full benefit of income splitting in your retirement years. Why does it take years? Suppose that a couple have yet to retire. One earns $80,000 per year and the other earns $24,000 a year from employment income. It's hard to shift employment income and thus, the higher-earner can't give it to his partner to save in his name or the tax will be attributed back to him. Thus, it often takes years of planning to effectively defeat the complex attribution tax rules.

Following the principles of cash management can transform your future. Learn to save. Pay yourself first. This may take a bit of getting used to, but it will benefit yourself and also everyone you care for. Remember to balance today and tomorrow. Both are important. Look ahead, and look more closely at the choices you make each day. Think about what you really want, not just now, but in the future, and don't lose sight of those goals under the pressures and desires of today. Be prepared, not just for hard times, but for good times too. Don't miss opportunities to make your life all that you want it to be.

14

Making Your Money Grow

Saving is your ticket to financial independence; you've accumulated enough capital to meet your future income requirements. But keep in mind that, over time, your ability to manage what you've saved will be as important as, if not more important than, your ability to save. How you manage your money will determine how it grows. Together, your cash management, tax management, and investment management decisions will determine how much capital you accumulate and, later in life, how much income you have, over and above pensions and government benefits, to maintain your lifestyle, to help educate your grandchildren, or buy that cabin on an island beach.

To make your money grow, you need to invest it. To ensure that your assets flourish, your financial plan should include an investment-management strategy. This strategy should provide a set of guidelines, based on your specific circumstances and goals, for all investment decisions you make now and in the future. This will ensure a consistent approach to the management of your portfolio and prevent unexpected, short-term market movements from distracting you from your long-term strategy. Your investment management strategy should reflect your risk tolerance and stated investment objectives, such as growth, income, or liquidity, and benchmarks to measure your annual performance. It should also be updated or reviewed whenever there are significant changes in your circumstances.

Many people feel apprehensive about investing, and indeed, with every kind of investment, there's some risk. Normally, as the level of risk increases, so does the possibility of earning higher returns. To make your money really grow, you need to place at least some of it in investments that offer the possibility of a superior rate of return (Table 3).

Effect of Rate of Return on Investment Growth (Table 3)

Investment Years	Average Return				
	4%	6%	8%	10%	12%
0	100,000	100,000	100,000	100,000	100,000
5	121,664	133,823	146,933	161,051	176,234
10	148,021	179,085	215,892	259,374	310,585
15	180,087	239,656	317,217	417,725	547,357
20	219,100	320,714	466,096	672,750	964,629
25	266,567	429,359	684,848	1,083,471	1,700,006

Investment risk can be managed effectively through adherence to some basic principles of investment management. Before making any investment decisions, you should have an understanding of the main components of investment risk, and you should consider your personal sensitivity to risk. This will help you choose investments that are right for you.

Your objectives for investment management will depend on your personal outlook, needs, financial goals, and risk tolerance. They should be compatible with your age and time horizon. They'll also change as you get older.

Mack and Deana, both 30 years old, had been saving on a regular basis since the age of 25. Their financial goals included retiring at 60. Because they'd begun saving at an early age, and had 30 years to fulfil their goal of retirement, their investment strategy required them to save less on annual basis then someone who was 40 years old. Secondly, because their investment time horizon was considered long-term, their investments were weighted more heavily in equities (investments offering the possibility of a higher return).

Colin and Nadine, in their 60s, were planning to retire in two years. Their financial plan confirmed that they could retire on an after-tax income of $60,000. Because they'd soon be drawing from the capital they'd saved, their investments were repositioned to a portfolio more heavily weighted in fixed-income (investments that may offer lower returns, but fluctuate less in value).

Types of Investment

Debt (Fixed-Income) Investments

When you loan your money based on the promise that you'll receive a fixed amount back, this is called a debt, or a fixed-income investment. Certificates of Deposit (CDs) and bonds are common examples of debt investments. When you invest your money in a fixed-income product, you're loaning it to the trust company or bank, which then pays you interest for the use of your money. This interest income is your reward for investing.

The financial institution, such as a bank or credit union, then loans your money to someone else at a higher interest rate. The financial institution makes its profits on the difference between what it pays you, and what it charges someone else. Similarly, when you buy a government bond, you loan your money to the government. In either case, there's a promise to pay you your money back at the time of maturity, plus the interest earned either monthly, quarterly or at the time of maturity.

Equity Investments

Equity investments represent a share of ownership in something. For example, common stock represents a share of ownership in a company. An equity mutual fund represents a share of ownership in many companies. The value of a stock, or an equity investment, may fluctuate. Unlike debt investments, equity investments are never fixed in value. They don't guarantee a specific return on your investment.

Risk

Investment risk is the degree of uncertainty of achieving an expected rate of return. Risk has many components and can wear many disguises. Every investment exposes you to one or more components of risk. The primary types of risk are inflation and variability.

Inflation

The main risk in fixed-income investments is quite subtle—loss of purchasing power caused by inflation. Many people invest in fixed income, because they like the idea of knowing, up front, what their reward for investing will be. But when you buy fixed-income products, once you subtract the taxes incurred on interest income and take inflation into account, your money may actually be shrinking.

Variability

When you purchase an equity investment, you're rewarded for assuming the risk that your investment may decline in value, but also has the potential for increasing in value, to a higher degree than a fixed-income investment. (Also, dividends and capital gains are taxed at a lower rate than interest income.)

The fluctuation in the value of an investment is referred to as variability. How much the value of an investment fluctuates is called its volatility. An asset with low volatility has historically fluctuated less than one with a high volatility. Two different investments with variability may have the same average long-term return, but different volatility ratings. The lower the volatility, the lower the chance of fluctuation in the value of an investment.

Comparing the Risks

Variability is the component of risk many investors fear most, but in fact, it's only a short-term risk, whereas inflation is a long-term risk, because inflation is constant. To measure the real rate of return of an investment, subtract the rate of inflation from the rate of return. Investments that are the most variable, such as equities, over the long-term, have far superior real rates of return than those of fixed value.

Lesley retired in 1977 with $500,000 in capital. This capital was to be used to supplement her government benefits and pension income. All her money was invested in fixed income. In her first year of retirement, she withdrew $16,000 of her investments to supplement her regular pension income. Due to inflation, each year she had to withdraw more of her money in order to maintain the same standard of living, and eventually this amount rose to over $51,000 by the year 2002 (the average inflation rate from 1977 to 2002 was 4.56%). Her capital was further decreased by the amount she had to withdraw each year to pay for income taxes (based on Marginal Tax Rates from 1978 to 2002). After only 25 years (1977 to 2002), her $500,000 had been consumed. Even though she received an average return of 8.60% on her investment (historical rate of return for fixed income from 1977 to 2002), inflation, and tax payable on interest income, had eroded those returns.

In the same year, 1977, Valerie invested her $500,000 investment capital in a good quality equity fund. Each year, Valerie withdrew the same amount as Lesley to supplement her retirement income. The value of her equity investment fluctuated each year: in some years, she made money; in others, she lost money. However, over the 25-year period, even after inflation, the average rate of return on her investment was 11.43%, and she'd paid proportionately less tax than Lesley, because of the lower tax rate for dividends and capital gains. After 25 years, Valerie still had nearly $300,000 of her original capital.

These examples, which are based on real economic data for the last 25 years, show that sometimes, in order to minimize the risk of not achieving your long-term financial objectives—such as having your money last as long as you do—you have to accept some short-term risk, namely the risk of variability. Does this mean you should put 100% of your money into equity investments? Absolutely not! However, a certain percentage of equities in an overall portfolio does make sense for most people.

Other Components of Risk

A risk with any type of investment is the risk of losing your capital. With equity investments, if the company goes broke, the stock becomes worthless, and your investment's worth nothing. (With equity investments in established companies, such as telephone companies or Coca-Cola, however, there's little risk of total loss of capital.) The same can happen with a debt investment. If the borrower (financial institution) goes broke, your debt investment becomes worthless, unless there was some other form of security such as FDIC (Federal Deposit Insurance Corporation). The majority of trust companies and bank institutions have FDIC insurance, but it's limited by institution to $100,000 per investor, determined by their Social Security number.

Some of the many other types of investment risk are:
- risk by industry sector;
- risk of currency fluctuation (on international investments);
- risk of marketability (lack of secondary market for trading);
- risk of poor results (selection without research or advice);
- risk of economic cycles (growth in gross domestic product or a recession);
- risk by geographic or political regions;
- risk of liquidity (the ability to quickly convert to cash);
- risk of reinvestment (lost opportunities while invested, and limited opportunities at maturity or disposition).

Managing Risk and Prospering

Since there's no such thing as a risk-free investment, it's important to manage that risk. Managing the various components of risk is best accomplished in four ways:
- diversifying your portfolio;
- maintaining a model asset allocation;
- using a contrarian investment approach;
- practicing due diligence.

Diversification

Diversification means not putting all your eggs in one basket. One way to diversify your portfolio is to have your investments distributed among the asset classes:

- cash;
- fixed-income;
- international fixed-income;
- US equities;
- international equities;
- real estate (real-estate investment trusts).

If your portfolio were 100% fixed-income and interest rates dropped, your whole portfolio would suffer. If your portfolio were 100% equity and equities were performing poorly, your whole portfolio would perform badly. In contrast, if you have a diversified portfolio, the likelihood that your whole portfolio will suffer, is reduced significantly.

Historically, when the rate of return increases on some asset classes, or on various other asset classes, the return tends to either increase, or decrease. This is referred to as correlation. For example, if the return on one asset class, such as US equities, increases, that of another asset class, such as international equities, will likely decrease. They move in opposite directions and thus are negatively correlated. An example of a positive correlation would be that, if international equities decrease, the US equities asset class would generally decrease as well.

By diversifying your portfolio with asset classes that are negatively correlated, you can reduce the overall risk of your portfolio. You might ask, how could a number of individual investments actually reduce the risk of a portfolio? Wouldn't the portfolio's risk level be the average risk level of each investment? Because of how the correlation of different asset classes works, this is not normally the case.

What is correlation anyway? It's a statistic that measures how one series of numbers interacts with another series of numbers. Simply put, correlation measures how much one investment goes up, when the other goes down.

For example, some international equities and US equities have a positive correlation to one another, and tend to move in the same direction. If you had an investment in each of these two classes, each investment would go up or down at the same time. If your portfolio consisted of only these international equities and US equities, since they're positively correlated, your whole portfolio would increase and decrease at the same time, thereby increasing your overall risk.

By contrast, having investments with a negative correlation is extremely beneficial. The investments would tend to go up and down at opposite times, decreasing overall risk. In other words, the negative returns of one equity would be offset by the positive returns of the other equity.

Diversifying your portfolio by using the right asset class combinations, allows you to hold assets that will tend to fluctuate in opposite directions, and thus your exposure to fluctuation in the value of your portfolio is reduced. In a perfectly negative correlation, risk would be eliminated completely; negative returns would be offset by positive returns. In the real world, this doesn't happen with perfect precision. Portfolios with different asset classes, will experience different patterns of returns for each asset class.

A Diversified Portfolio (Figure 1)

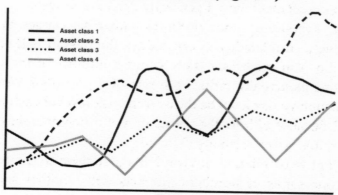

Time

Figure 1 shows hypothetical returns from investments in four different asset classes; the asset classes don't always move in the same direction at the same time, and the risk level (volatility) of the portfolio is lower than with fewer classes, but it hasn't been completely eliminated. Knowing how different investments react to different circumstances is the foundation of diversification, and the basis for determining the correlation between investments. You can't diversify properly if you don't know how investments move in relation to one another. Rest assured, a good financial advisor can help you determine how your portfolio should be diversified. Today's methodology will typically involve the use of the Nobel Prize-winning investment research of Markowitz and Sharpe, called the Efficient Frontier. To underscore the importance of getting the right asset allocation, research studies have found that a very high percentage of the return people get on their investments isn't the result of the specific investments they hold, but rather the combination of asset classes in their portfolios. What we're saying here is that the asset allocation may be even more important than individual investment selection.

In reviewing your portfolio's performance, always remember to look at the whole portfolio rather than focusing on one particular asset class. Individual investments will move up and down quite a bit, whereas the average return of the investments combined won't be as volatile. (See Figure 1.) Diversification reduces the risk of the portfolio as a whole, but not the risk of the individual investments. Don't panic if just one component of your portfolio is doing poorly.

Ways to Diversify

If your investment assets are relatively small, it can be difficult to achieve adequate diversification through direct ownership of each of the various types of assets, but acquiring these assets through mutual fund companies, or an asset management service, makes diversification possible for even the smallest investor (see Table 4).

A Diversified $100,000 Portfolio (Table 4)

Amount	Investment	Holding Within Fund
$5,000	Money market fund	T-bills and CDs
$20,000	Bond fund	High-quality government and corporate bonds
$10,000	International bond fund	High-quality international bonds
$20,000	US equity fund	Shares in established US companies
$35,000	International equity fund	Shares in established companies worldwide
$10,000	Real estate	Real estate investment trust

Maintaining a Model Asset Allocation

In a model asset allocation, such as that shown in Table 4, a portion of your portfolio is kept in each of the asset classes. The desired percentage for each asset class is set according to your timeframe, your personal goals, and risk tolerance. The average rate of return for a given asset class over many decades indicates, with reasonable certainty, what return these assets are likely to produce over the long-term. To maintain balance in your portfolio, sell investments in any asset class that exceed the predetermined percentage and buy investments in those classes that drop below their set percentages. This forces you to buy low and sell high. Maintaining a model asset allocation is one way to lock in the gains your portfolio experiences. A knowledgeable financial advisor can identify specific assets for each asset class, as well as the model allocation most appropriate for you.

Contrarian Investment Approach

Contrarians go against current trends. Given an investment that continues to experience superior returns, the normal inclination is to hold onto it, or buy more of that investment. Before you know it, it shrinks in value. Using a contrarian approach, you'd sell when the investment is high, to cash in on your profits, and buy another investment that's low. Unfortunately, most investors, and even many investment advisors, do just the opposite.

Maintaining a model asset allocation, and balancing your portfolio on a regular basis, forces you to realize your profits. If an asset class increases in value beyond a planned, stated percentage, you sell it, locking in your profits, and invest in asset classes that are underachieving. While this approach takes discipline, the long-term investor adhering to this strategy will certainly be rewarded.

This is what pension fund managers have done for years, and what, in recent years, personal investment advisors have done. Sharp investors have caught on and are copying this always-successful portfolio-management strategy. In fact, most good advisors will routinely rebalance an investor's portfolio as part of their services.

Due Diligence

Another way to mitigate investment risk, is by selecting quality assets with intrinsic value. To achieve this, you need a well-defined process for selecting investments. Due diligence is often the most difficult aspect of the whole investment process, because there are so many investment options available. An experienced financial advisor can help in your selection process. It's much easier to choose one experienced, knowledge-able advisor, than to continually pick good investments. It's also far less time-consuming.

Investment Management Points to Remember

• Know yourself

To make an investment without having a clear understanding of your goals and objectives, would be like putting the cart before the horse. It's also important to evaluate your risk sensitivity, and ensure you understand the various components of risk of a given investment, before committing to it.

• Minimize the risk of not achieving long-term financial objectives

Consider the financial risk of falling short of meeting financial objectives. In order to minimize this long-term risk, the risk of running out of money, investors must accept some short-term risks of having the value of some of their investments fluctuate.

• Use diversification to build an investment portfolio that minimizes risk

Build a well-diversified portfolio, since this type of portfolio has the best potential for enhanced returns, with less risk over the long-term.

• Maintain a model asset allocation strategy

Decide on a model allocation that suits your personal goals, risk sensitivity, and timeframe. A diverse set of asset classes should be selected to minimize investment risk. The asset mix will determine the long-term risk, and return characteristics of the portfolio as a whole. Balance your portfolio periodically to maintain your predetermined percentage returns.

• Exercise due diligence in selecting quality investments within each asset class

An experienced financial advisor can help you select high quality investments, appropriate for each asset class in your portfolio.

Seeking top quality professional advice shouldn't cost anything. In fact, it should pay. The benefits of good advice should always outweigh the costs. A good advisor should identify investments that best match your specific personal requirements.

Julia and Andreas had always invested in fixed-income products. Currently, their fixed-income product portfolio was valued at $600,000. It averaged a return of 5.0%. With their annual interest income of $30,000, their company pensions, and government benefits, their marginal tax rate was 37%. They were paying over $11,000 in tax on the interest they earned on their fixed-income products. Their financial advisor developed an investment strategy to reduce their taxes, by reducing the fixed-income component of their portfolio to 40% and allocating the remainder among other assets classes (cash, equities, real estate). Although their portfolio now included an equity component, their actual investment risk was reduced, because their portfolio was more efficiently allocated, and they had less exposure to inflation and rate-of-return risk. Andreas and Julia would now be able to save $6,000 in tax each year, while continuing to maintain a conservative portfolio. Their advisor told them that based on historical returns of the last 50 years, their average annual return for their asset allocation would now be 7.74%.

15

Protecting Yourself and Your Family

Financial security means different things to different people, at each stage of life, but it matters to everyone.

Cheryl and Jack, in their early 30s, both work full-time to provide for their family of four. To them, financial security means having enough money to pay the monthly bills, buy groceries, pay for daycare, and provide clothing and shelter.

Cameron and Nora are in their late 50s. To them, financial security means that, upon retirement, they'll be able to maintain their current standard of living and travel once a year.

Saul and Abby, in their late 60s, want to ensure that, in the event that one of them requires 24-hour care due to age or illness, the other will still be able to stay active in the things they enjoy. To them, financial security means having the resources to hire help if needed.

In its fullest sense, to be financially secure is to be confident that you can cope with any financial emergencies or unexpected expenses that may come up and still maintain your customary lifestyle. It is to feel secure about the future.

If you died tomorrow, would the loss of your income create financial hardship for members of your family or other dependents? If you experienced a permanent disability, or were diagnosed with a critical illness, would your current resources provide the needed assistance for your care and the care of your family? If your spouse or partner required long-term, 24-hour care, could you or your family afford the time or money to provide it? In reality, no one can feel absolutely certain of his or her future needs or financial resources, but you can mitigate your exposure to these types of risks.

Until you've created sufficient wealth to provide adequate income for your dependents in the event of your death, disability, critical illness, or need for long-term care, it's vital to manage these risks. In fact, doing so is one of the keys to preserving wealth.

Principles of Risk Management

Here's how to reduce your exposure to the chance of loss.

• Insure your income

If your earned income is necessary to attain financial independence, or for your family's security, and if it's possible for you to do so, acquire insurance coverage to insure your income.

- **Insure your life**

If loss of income through premature death would pose a threat to your family's financial security, transfer that risk to an insurance company by acquiring life insurance.

- **Insure your property**

Insure against the chance of major property loss, such as your home, cottage, cars, and other prized personal possessions. Even minor losses that can be insured for a reasonable amount, should be.

- **Insure against contingent liabilities**

Eliminate chances of loss that would impair your ability to attain, or retain, your financial independence. This can be accomplished through a combination of homeowner insurance, auto insurance, and professional liability insurance, if applicable.

- **Insure against major medical expenses**

Long-Term Care Insurance Plans help protect your savings and preserve your personal freedom to choose where and how you receive long-term care services. It helps pay for home care, whether provided by family and friends or through professional home-care organizations. It also helps cover care received in Adult Day Care, Assisted Living Facilities, and Nursing Homes. With a flexible product design, you can structure a plan that's right for you and meets your specific needs and budget. In a time when people are increasingly worried about providing care services for themselves, their spouses or other family members, Long-Term Care Plans are designed to help take the worry out of long-term care planning.

Risk management means anticipating potential losses, knowing your options in advance, and ensuring you have the necessary resources to help cover those losses. To design a risk-management strategy that suits your situation, follow the steps below.

1. Identify the potential risks.

2. Evaluate the effects of each risk.

3. Determine how to manage each risk; eliminate, reduce, retain, or transfer it.

4. Select the correct insurance coverage.

What Are the Risks?

Most people are insured against at least some kinds of loss. It's usual to have house, car, or personal belongings insurance. Insurance against personal liability for an injury caused to someone else—someone who slips on your steps or runs in front of your car, for example—is also common. Insurance covering medical expenses incurred outside the country, is obtained as a matter of course by most people who travel regularly. Insuring yourself against these risks is always wise.

A less often recognized, but potentially even more devastating loss—one that, as long as you're working, you risk each day—is loss of income caused by a disability producing sickness or injury, a critical illness, or premature death (see Table 5). Unless you're already financially independent, you depend on your income to sustain you and those you love. To earn that income, you need to be healthy. But accidents do happen and people do get sick. Consider for a moment what the loss to you and your family would be, if you could no longer work, perhaps not for years, starting today.

Value of Ability to Earn Income* (Table 5)

Monthly Income	Years Left to Work		
	10	20	30
$2,500	$396,203	$1,041,577	$2,092,823
$5,000	$792,407	$2,083,155	$4,185,647
$7,500	$1,188,610	$3,124,732	$6,278,471
$10,000	$1,584,814	$4,166,310	$8,371,294

* Assumes 5% inflationary/promotional increases each year.

Disability

What are your chances of actually suffering a loss of income as a result of a disability before you reach age 65? Your odds of being off for more than 90 days are about 50/50 (see Table 6). How long might you remain unable to work? The average time lost due to sickness and injury, including permanent disability, is more than two years. Fortunately, the chance of loss of income through disability is an insurable risk, with some limitations.

The Chances of Being Disabled (Table 6)

Your Age	Chance of being disabled longer than 90 days	Average years of disability after 90 days
25	58%	1.2
30	54%	2.5
35	50%	2.8
40	45%	3.1
45	40%	3.2
50	30%	3.1
55	25%	2.6
60	14%	1.6

Source: 1985 Commissioner's IDA Morbidity and Commissioner's SO Mortality Tables, Society of Actuaries

Critical Illness

When you're healthy, you rarely, if ever, think about being diagnosed with a life-changing illness. But at some point in your life, you may well face this challenge. The good news is, improved medicines and treatments, mean that today, people diagnosed with a critical illness generally recover and, in time, get on with their lives. Not having the financial resources to pay for the unexpected costs of illness, however, can destroy a family's future.

Preventing And Controlling Cancer

We don't know exactly why people get cancer. Nor do we have a cure.

What researchers do know is that doing certain things, like exercising regularly and eating a healthy diet—and not doing others, like smoking or sunbathing—can reduce our cancer risk. And getting regular screenings, or tests, can help find cancer early, making treatment easier and more likely to succeed.

Healthy Lifestyle

Researchers continue to study how our lifestyles and environment affect our cancer risk. One area of interest and concern is the link between being overweight and developing cancer. Research shows that about one-third of all cancer deaths are related to diet and lack of physical activity in adults, according to the American Cancer Society.

Age and family history also can put you at greater risk for some kinds of cancer. While we can't do anything about those, we can control or change our lifestyles. Here are some things the Oncology Nursing Society and other health groups say you can do to lower your risk for cancer:

• Eat a healthy diet that is easy on red meat and saturated fats and rich in whole grains, fruit, and vegetables, especially those that are dark green, deep yellow, and orange. Limit foods that are smoked, salt-cured, or preserved with nitrites. Remove skin from poultry and fat from meat. Choose natural foods, such as raw nuts, raisins, or bran cereal, over highly processed foods, such as sugared cereals, chips, cookies, and other snack foods.

• Get at least 30 minutes of physical activity at least five times a week.

- Maintain a healthy weight.
- Don't smoke and avoid places where people are smoking.
- Drink alcohol moderately (one drink daily for women, two for men).
- Wear sunscreen and avoid direct sun when it's strongest (10 a.m. to 4 p.m.)
- Avoid other kinds of radiation (tanning salons) and substances that can cause cancer, like radon and asbestos.

Early Detection

We also can be responsible for getting tests to find cancer early. There are several screening tests for different cancers, including:

- breast
- prostate
- cervical
- colon
- ovarian
- skin

You should talk with your doctor about which tests to have and how often. Find out what the test involves and what you need to do to prepare. Based on your family and personal health history, your doctor might recommend a different schedule for some tests than the one outlined for other people your age.

If you're age 50 or older, here are some of the cancer tests you should know about:

Breast Cancer

You should have a mammogram, an x-ray to help find breast cancer when a growth is too small to feel, every year. You also should perform monthly breast self-examinations and have a yearly breast exam done by a health professional.

Cervical Cancer

A Pap test can find pre-cancer cells in the cervix or vagina. You should have this test at least once every three years. If you're past age 65, you might be able to stop having the test, depending on your medical history.

Prostate Cancer

If you're a man, talk to your doctor about having an annual prostate-specific antigen (PSA) blood test and digital rectal examination (DRE). Ask about the pros and cons of getting tested at your age.

Colon Cancer

Men and women should have one or more of the following tests for colon cancer:
- sigmoidoscopy
- yearly stool blood test
- barium enema
- colonoscopy

Skin Cancer

You should have a routine skin checkup every year. Doctors can see most signs of skin cancer with the naked eye. As they check your skin, they will look for anything abnormal or unusual, like lumps or discolored or odd-shaped moles.

Ovarian Cancer

If you're a woman, talk to your doctor about screening for ovarian cancer. Screening tools include a blood test, ultrasound, and pelvic exam. Because ovarian cancer is so hard to find early, ask your doctor how to recognize symptoms of the disease.

Eating well, getting enough sleep and exercise, and controlling your weight and stress can help prevent illness and improve your health overall. Right now, living a healthy lifestyle, along with tests to catch cancer early, is your best defense against the disease.

The older you get, the more likely you are to encounter serious medical problems—cancer, heart disease and strokes, and Alzheimer's. Critical illness insurance can relieve some of the financial stress caused by illness, allowing you more choices in treatment, and leaving you free to focus on recovering.

What is Long-Term Care?
The Need for Long-Term Care

Long-term care refers to a broad range of supportive medical, personal and social services needed by people who are unable to meet their basic living needs for an extended period of time. This may be caused by accident, illness or frailty. Such conditions include the inability to move about, dress, bathe, eat, use a toilet, medicate and avoid incontinence. Also, care may be needed to help the disabled with household cleaning, preparing meals, shopping, paying bills, visiting the doctor, answering the phone and taking medications. Additional long-term care needs may be the result of cognitive impairment from stroke, depression, dementia, Alzheimer's, Parkinson's and so on.

Long-term care support can be provided either at home or in an alternate care facility. As a rule, those who need long-term care prefer to stay at home and most of the time so-called informal care givers (family and friends) prefer the home as well. The deciding factor of where to receive help ultimately centers on the nature of the need. For example, a wife caring for her overweight husband may be unable to help him bathe, dress, use the toilet, or even transfer him from the bed to a chair. She will either have to hire aides to come to the home or consider an alternate care facility, such as a nursing home. Another example might be an Alzheimer's patient who has become unmanageable and must receive constant supervision. This may be impossible at home and an Alzheimer's facility may be the only solution.

Facts About Long-term Care

The nature of long-term care in our society is changing. Medical science is keeping us alive longer and there are fewer early sudden deaths. Fewer deaths mean more prolonged health problems requiring long-term care. In fact, the average life span for people born in 1900 was 47 years and for those born in 1940, it is more than 80 years. In addition, the population of those over age 65 is increasing while the younger population is stagnating. The aging trend will continue until at least 2030 when the last baby boomers enter the 65+ group. With this in mind, it is important to realize that the odds of entering a nursing home and staying there for an extended period of time, increase with age. In fact, statistics show that at any given time, 22% of those aged 85 and older are in a nursing home. One in two persons over age 85 need long-term care. Between ages 65 to 74, 12% of all people need help with the tasks of daily living. At age 85 and older, 70% of all people need such assistance.

Today, family members and friends are the sole caregivers for 70% of the seniors receiving long-term care. However, changes in the family structure are leading to more nursing home stays than ever before. The support provided by traditional care givers is becoming less available. Every year more and more women are entering the workforce due to an increase in single parent households and due to increased income needs of dual parent households. Also, people are having fewer children thus, affecting the future supply of care givers. And finally, many family members are moving away and are unable to help because they don't live close by. These are all factors that reduce the pool of available care givers. And this lack of traditional family care givers is forcing more people to spend out-of-pocket for the services of paid professionals or, for so-called formal care.

In 2000, $137 billion was spent on long-term care for all ages. As the baby boomers get older, this amount will increase dramatically. It is estimated that spending on long-term care for just seniors will increase to $379 billion by 2050.

No longer can most people fund long-term care out of their retirement income or savings. In 2000, the average cost of nursing home care in the United States was $153 per day, ranging from $90 to $295. The average cost per year was $55,000, which means that the average nursing home stay (2.5 years) costs $137,000. Not only have the costs of long-term care increased, but because of supply and demand they will probably increase at a greater rate than inflation. In fact, the costs of long-term care will more than quadruple by 2030. Thus, one must be concerned and plan for the present high costs of long-term care, knowing that the costs will be much higher later.

The Crisis in Long-term Care
We are facing a potential future crisis in long-term care, and so far, the government has shown little inclination to provide a long-term care entitlement program that is similar to Social Security and Medicare. With increasing pressure from the AARP and the demands of a voting public that is increasingly growing older, the government's attitude may change. Government programs may take one, or a combination of the

two approaches. The first might be a national long-term care insurance program funded jointly by the government, employers and insured individuals. The second might be government support of private LTC insurance. But since not all people can qualify for individual long-term care insurance because of poor health, the government might encourage the establishment of employer group plans in a system similar to the private offering of health insurance through employers. There may be other approaches as well, but it is probably a sure bet the government will eventually intervene in solving a pending long-term care crisis.

Some individuals may be able to rely on other family members for support, but with the demands of everyday living, fewer people are able to devote the hours required to provide long-term care to loved ones. A family member may have to quit his or her job to provide care, or sacrifice savings to pay for it.

For many seniors, the private sector has enabled them to have a much better quality of life, whether they live at home, or choose to go into a managed care facility. Planning ahead for the eventual cost of long-term care is wise; sometimes, private care is the only real option. Long-term care coverage is designed to address the health, social, and personal needs of people who've lost the capability of caring for themselves. It can help bridge the gap between the government subsidy you receive, and the extra care or services you might require or prefer.

Premature Death

When a parent, spouse, or partner dies prematurely, the loss of his or her income to family members can extend the trauma far into the future. This potential loss is an insurable risk.

Life insurance is for the unexpected. It's for the people you leave behind. It's not about getting rich, but about allowing your family and loved ones to carry on without financial hardship.

When you're younger, the odds that you'll die soon are lower than when you're older. But it's also a time when you have various financial obligations, such as a mortgage, personal debt, and the costs of educating your children. If you were to die prematurely, would your spouse or partner be able to afford these costs? Would your family have to reduce their quality of lifestyle, or depend on other family members, to help them get by?

If you have a financially-dependent elder parent, relative, or friend, how will they fare if you're suddenly gone? Are there others with sufficient financial resources who'd be willing to step in?

If you have dependents of any kind, you need to consider whether your current financial resources would be sufficient to meet the income needs of surviving family members.

As you grow older, the need for life insurance changes, and the major concern becomes estate preservation and taxes. If you have enough capital to continue supporting your family's lifestyle, while paying tax and estate costs, and if leaving your estate intact for your heirs is not of high importance, then life insurance probably isn't for you. But if maximizing your estate is important, insurance can meet this need. If you don't have a lot of assets to pass on as an inheritance, life insurance can be used to create a legacy for your loved ones. A financial advisor can provide you with more information about using life insurance for estate and tax purposes.

Are You Covered?
Capital Analysis in the Event of Death

A capital analysis in the event of death will tell you if your current financial resources will be sufficient to meet the income needs of surviving family members, or if insurance coverage is required. This isn't always easy to determine, and a qualified financial advisor should do this analysis.

222 *The Retirement Guide*

The analysis should use a worst-case scenario, and assume death occurs tomorrow. The first step is to identify the net present value of all sources of capital at the time of death. These include:

• survivor benefits available to children under various government programs;

• Social Security survivor benefits available to spouse;

• Social Security (regular) benefits payable to a working spouse;

• Old Age Security (OAS) benefits payable to spouse;

• spouse's employment income until retirement;

• spouse's pension benefits payable after retirement;

• net invested assets, as well as the income from these assets, throughout spouse's lifetime;

• survivor benefits under company pension plan that will be payable to spouse;

• life insurance from group and personally held plans;

• other sources of capital, such as the sale of a cottage, or even of your current home, if downsizing is appropriate.

Once the value of your revenue streams is known, your financial advisor will subtract the tax payable to determine the income your family can anticipate in the event of your death.

You now must identify the capital needs of your family. This calculation is based primarily on the cost of the lifestyle you'd like your dependants to have in the event of your death. Some of the needs routinely addressed are:

• final expenses;

• income taxes payable;

• repayment of outstanding loans;

• after-tax income required before retirement;

• after-tax income required after retirement;

• childcare and housekeeping replacement;

• educational capital to provide for each child's post secondary educational needs;

• special bequests (i.e., charities).

If the calculation shows an estate surplus, you have more money than is required to meet the objectives you've set out for your dependants. Thus, you can increase your objectives, or decrease your life insurance. Alternatively, if there's a shortfall, you need to reduce your objectives, or apply for more life insurance. Now, you're in a good position to decide which type of life insurance is most appropriate for your situation (see Appendix A: Types of Insurance). If insurance isn't available to you because of health impairments, your financial advisor will assist you in devising a strategy to reduce the objectives for your family to help minimize the potential financial hardship.

Dorie and Greg were in their late 40s. A capital analysis in the event of death revealed that, in the event of Dorie's premature death, there'd be a shortage of approximately $300,000. Because Greg didn't work outside the home or earn an income, there was no financial shortage in the event of his death. Since this was a temporary need that would gradually be eliminated as they approached retirement at age 65, they purchased a 20-year term insurance policy in the amount of $300,000.

Brian and Dylan's financial advisor determined that, on the death of the second spouse, the income and capital gains tax owing, would significantly reduce the value of their estate. They wanted their children to have a sizable legacy, so they purchased a joint second-to-die term to 100 insurance policy, that would pay on the death of the second spouse, in the amount of the approximate tax payable at second death. The proceeds of the policy would go toward paying any tax and estate costs, leaving their estate intact.

Louis and Joanna's financial plan revealed more than $200,000 in their estate that wasn't needed to meet their objectives. Since they wouldn't be spending this capital in their lifetime, they decided to maximize their estate by transferring some of their investment assets to a universal life policy, to be invested in either a fixed-income product account or mutual fund portfolio. By doing so, they reduced their annual taxes (less capital gains and interest income would be attributed to them on an annual basis), reduced future estate taxation (since the death benefit would be paid tax free), and maximized their estate to their beneficiaries (since the funds in the policy would grow tax free).

Capital Analysis in the Event of Need for Long-Term Care

Planning for long-term care, is somewhat more complex than planning for death. You're either dead or alive, but with long-term care, it's a matter of degree. How long you will need assistance, will depend on what caused, or is causing, the need for care. How long you need long-term care will depend on your medical condition and age. Unlike someone who dies, someone who has become disabled, or incapable of self-care, will continue to consume, continue to require care, and may even require special equipment, which can be expensive.

A capital analysis should be conducted by your financial advisor, determining if your current financial resources will be sufficient to maintain an acceptable standard of living in the event you require long-term care. A long-term care analysis should determine if your current resources are sufficient to cover increased costs to pay for home or facility care. The difference between the money available, and the money needed, will result in either a capital surplus, or a capital shortfall, at the time the care is required. The objectives routinely addressed in an analysis for disability and long-term care include:

- after-tax income required before retirement;
- after-tax income required after retirement;
- income taxes payable;
- educational capital to provide for each child's post secondary educational needs;
- ongoing payment of existing mortgages and loans;
- amount of homecare required;
- amount of facility care required.

Any shortage identified will lessen over time, and may even disappear, as you get closer to achieving financial independence. However, the need for long-term care earlier in life can reduce your ability to achieve financial independence in the future. By contrast, your risk of requiring long-term care, increases as you age, and never completely disappears.

Choosing the right type of long-term care insurance is complex (see Appendix A: Types of Insurance). However, the decision becomes easier when you know how much you need, the maximum amount you can buy, and how much you can afford, without having a detrimental effect on your personal cash flow. Acquiring the coverage that's right for you, will give you peace of mind and ensure a more secure future for both yourself and your family.

16

Planning Your Estate

Your estate is your collective assets and any related liabilities. Estate planning is the art of designing a plan for the effective enjoyment, ownership, management, and disposition of your assets, during life, upon death, and after death, at the minimal amount of tax. Many believe that estate planning is only for those of advanced age or approaching death. But whatever your age, estate planning shouldn't be ignored. It's an essential part of the financial-planning process.

Your estate plan should include a current will outlining how you'd like your assets distributed when you die; Powers of Attorney for property and personal care in the event you become incapacitated; and, possibly, various other strategies to fulfill your wishes while you're still alive.

The estate-planning process requires advisors who possess considerable skill and knowledge. They must combine technical expertise with sensitivity to your individual circumstances. To create an effective estate plan, your advisors must take into account your personality, your specific goals and objectives, priorities and preferences, and your personal relationships.

The fundamental objective of estate planning is to nurture wealth-building in your own individual estate, while minimizing the overall tax burden for all members of your family. Since the exposure of assets to excessive taxation can prevent the accomplishment of desired objectives and bring hardship to a family, estate planning can be even more important to the owner of a medium-sized estate than to the owner of a large estate.

Common Goals of Estate Planning

The goals of estate planning affect three important areas:
1. Estate creation: preserve and maximize the legacy that will pass to your heirs.
2. Estate distribution: distribute assets in accordance with your wishes in the most efficient manner possible.
3. Estate tax reduction: reduce waste by minimizing the expenses and taxes on the transfer of your wealth.
4. Estate tax payment: pay unavoidable expenses and taxes on transfer of wealth in the most economical fashion possible.

• Maintain family harmony

Nearly everyone knows of a case of disrupted family relations, precipitated by changing events at the death of a family member. Such circumstances are typically due to lack of estate planning.

Conflict can also occur while you're alive, if assets are given or sold to one or more family members to the exclusion of others. An example would be if you gave a less-fortunate family member assistance to make a down payment on his or her first home, but didn't offer similar assistance or some form of compensation to other family members. To avoid conflict in such circumstances, compassion must be exercised in a discreet manner.

A well-intentioned, but poorly drafted and executed estate plan, can create emotional scars. A classic example is the bequest of the family cottage to one child and the investment portfolio to a second child: at the time the will is drafted, both the cottage and investment portfolio have similar values; at the time of death, their values are vastly different. Good planning doesn't leave intentions and fairness to chance.

• Minimize taxes

Taxes on an estate can be minimized in a variety of ways. Income-splitting between spouses, children, or members of the extended family, such as grandchildren, nieces, and nephews, is effective in some situations. Estate freezes can be used to transfer future growth in certain assets to the next generation, which can maximize estate values by deferring capital-gains taxes. Certain rollover provisions can also be used to conserve an estate at death and defer tax liabilities. For example, IRAs and capital assets can roll automatically to the surviving spouse, and assets not qualified for rollover can be bequeathed to other beneficiaries.

• Preserve the estate or avert a liquidity crisis

Emergencies while you're still alive, or the taxes triggered by the disposition of assets upon death, can create a liquidity crisis. This can force the sale of invested assets at an inopportune time or at depressed values, to create needed cash. If you don't plan ahead to create flexibility and ensure accessible cash for contingencies, a portion of your estate could be needlessly wiped out.

• Keep assets in the family

Assets with sentimental as well as material value, such as a cottage or family business, often have to be sold against the wishes of the family, either prior to or after the owner's death, in order to provide the needed cash to pay taxes, cover final expenses, and fulfill other bequests. Estate planning can help prevent such situations.

• **Provide for the financial security of survivors and loved ones**

Life insurance can be used to create immediate capital at death and offset the lost income of a testator. Trusts can be used to conserve existing capital until designated disposition dates. Trusts and life interests can also be used to provide continual funds for certain beneficiaries while alive, with the assets remaining passed to another beneficiary.

• **Judgement-proof assets**

Judgement- and creditor-proofing assets in the estate, in order to protect them against malpractice lawsuits, litigations, and creditors, is often a concern and goal for professional practitioners or business owners.

• **Bypass probate**

In recent years, probate fees—a form of administrative tax on an estate levied by the state government at death—have increased dramatically. Probate fees are calculated based on the gross value of your assets, not the net value.

For some types of assets, probate fees can be reduced through joint ownership. With joint ownership, the asset doesn't form part of the estate, since the ownership passes to the surviving joint owner at the moment of death. This tactic must be used with care, to avoid unwanted taxes accruing to the joint owner and other potential problems.

Harry and Judith were in their early 60s and had been retired for five years. To provide a guaranteed income each month, they invested their resources exclusively in fixed-income products. On the interest income they received, they found they could barely get by. But they wanted to ensure that their children receive some type of inheritance upon their death, so they placed half of each of their fixed accountss in joint registration with their children. By investing only in fixed income, they were paying far more tax each year than they would using other investment strategies that could provide a guaranteed higher annual net-after-tax income, and still allow their children to enjoy the full value of their estate.

More importantly, they didn't realize that they had potentially reduced the future income available to a surviving spouse. On the death of either of them, the joint registration with their children of half their investments would override any provisions made in their wills. In the future, one of them might be in the potentially awkward position of having to ask his or her children to return money.

For certain assets, such as life insurance proceeds and pension plans, the use of directly named beneficiaries can also avert probate.

• Preserve business assets

The mere existence of a business adds to the complexity of an estate. For most successful business owners, the business represents a significant asset, and an orderly succession is critical to preserving the value of the business as a going concern. Estate issues for business owners include control of the business, providing for survivors, retirement, and permitting family or outsiders to participate in the business. Without an estate plan, the surviving family members of the business owner may be faced with a financial crisis, due to their lack of knowledge of the affairs of the business. Planning shouldn't be restricted to family members, but should include financial, legal, and accounting advisors, as well as managers, executors, and trustees.

Estate Planning in General

Estate plans range from a simple will, to complex trusts, and the use of holding companies. Other progressive planning strategies involve reduction or elimination of capital gains, estate freezes, transfers or gifts of properties, use of direct beneficiaries outside the estate, joint title or life interest in properties, offshore trusts, and spousal trusts. Effective estate planning requires the advice of specialists from many fields, including taxation, estate law, family law, and insurance. Each case is unique. No factor should be dealt with in isolation.

A complete understanding of the relevant facts, as well as the needs and intentions of the individual and the family, are essential preliminary steps in developing an estate plan (see the Estate Planning Checklist in Appendix B).

In formulating an estate plan, you need to develop a framework for decision making and subsequent action. Without such a framework, you could end up receiving conflicting recommendations from various advisors. With a financial advisor coordinating the development and implementation of your estate plan, the task becomes much less onerous.

Once your estate plan is completed, it should be reviewed periodically to ensure that changing circumstances in the extended family unit, such as divorce or remarriage, will not result in unintended beneficiaries. A review is also recommended after any significant tax-law changes.

The information provided in this chapter is intended only to increase your awareness of estate planning. You should consult your financial advisor, or other professional advisors, for individual recommendations and advice on estate planning issues.

Avoiding Common Pitfalls in Estate Planning

1. "I've Done It All"

The number one mistake made by most Americans is that if they have a will or trust they feel their estate planning is complete and nothing else needs to be done. This causes untold disasters. Why is that? Most Americans are conscientious and want to take care of their financial matters, but they see their financial issues as separate and isolated. For example, they see their income tax planning as having no impact on their estate planning. They see their retirement planning as separate and distinct from their form of business organization. In reality every area of a person's financial life is interconnected with every other area. The problem is that you cannot see that interconnection until a major event occurs, and then it's too late.

2. "You're In The Middle"

The second common problem is that individuals are put in the unenviable position of being in the middle, and normally have to initiate the questions to the experts and professionals. In most cases they don't know what questions to ask, or even worse, the question arises out of an unfortunate event that has just occurred. In addition, they probably are not knowledgeable, experienced or informed on how one issue may affect another issue in the overall financial plan.

3. "Advisors Don't Communicate With Each Other"

Of course you surround yourself with knowledgeable professionals, but unfortunately they often operate in a vacuum. The result is that their advice is delivered from their perspective without any regard to the other advisor's advice.

To prevent this problem, you will require a strong financial advisor. The financial advisor should have knowledge and experience/contacts in the areas of law, taxation, insurance and investments should be tasked to act as the coordinator for your financial estate plan.

Steps to an effective financial/estate plan.
1. You can only have one major goal in life.
2. Once that is determined (and that must be determined first) all other decisions regarding taxes, retirement plans, business agreements, etc. need to be tested as to "how do they impact that goal." The question you always need to ask yourself is how does this decision help me achieve my major goal.
3. Have your financial advisor do a "reality test." A "reality test" is defined as "taking everything in your financial life as it exists today and test it through several scenarios: 1) while everyone involved is alive; 2) if you are married, when one of you dies; and 3) when both of you pass".
Once you have completed the reality test this will uncover the inter-connection between all aspects of your financial life and will expose any potential undesirable results.
4. Now as you move forward in your planning with your advisors, continue to evaluate their suggestions by how their specific recommendations interact with the other financial areas in your life, and specifically how do the recommendations help achieve that major goal.

If a decision or a recommendation is in conflict or doesn't help you achieve your major goal, don't do it.

17

Choosing a Financial Advisor

Throughout this book we've used the term financial advisor in reference to the person from whom you receive various types of financial advice. We now need to get more specific.

In choosing an advisor, you need to first determine the type of advice you're looking for. Do you require specific investment advice, or a more comprehensive level of service including advice on other issues, such as tax and estate matters? Are you looking for someone specializing in family situations or inter-generational planning? Perhaps you hope to find an advisor who can address senior care issues, help you deal with seniorly parents, and act as a family advisor.

If you're only looking for investment recommendations, then an investment advisor might be right for your situation. However, be aware that an investment advisor's specialty is investments, and he or she may not typically practice more comprehensive financial planning. Their recommendations, no matter how objective, may not take into account other issues that could well have an impact on your investment decisions. If you're seeking someone to fit all the pieces together, then a financial advisor who can provide comprehensive advice is the right person for you. This person we refer to as a Registered Investment Advisor ("RIA") or a Certified Financial Planner ("CFP").

If your advisor doesn't have the requisite experience or qualifications to provide recommendations in a particular area in which you need advice—for example, taxes or estate planning—they should inform you of this and direct you to a qualified person who can address your concerns. Ideally, a CFP or RIA should be the key person who designs a cohesive plan to meet your financial goals and then works, either alone or with other specialists, to implement the various elements of your plan.

Your planner should first guide you in gathering information on your whole financial situation and estimating income needs and expenses. He or she will need you to describe your financial and personal goals and objectives, as well as your personal values and attitudes. (This information is part of your life plan). With this information in hand, your financial advisor should either do or facilitate the following for you:

• identify financial problems that may prevent you from attaining your stated goals;

• provide written recommendations and alternative solutions to meet your needs;

• develop a strategy to minimize tax payable now and in the future;

• design a personal investment strategy suited to your situation, taking into account your investment risk tolerance;

• plan for life changes that will affect your finances, such as the death of a spouse, or failing health;

- review your will and Powers of Attorney;
- put your estate in order and plan for a tax-effective transfer of your assets to your beneficiaries upon your death;
- assist in implementing strategies to meet your stated goals, either directly, or by putting you in touch with the appropriate, knowledgeable professional;
- work with other professional advisors, such as your lawyer and accountant;
- regularly review your financial plan and make appropriate revisions, as dictated by any changing personal, economic, or other circumstances.

Professional Qualifications

Certified Financial Planners must meet a set of standards in the areas of education, ethics, experience, and examination, set forth by the Financial Planners Standards Council ("FPSC"). The FPSC is a not-for-profit organization established in 1995 to benefit the public and the financial planning profession by establishing and enforcing competency and ethical standards for financial planners who hold the designation of Certified Financial Planner ("CFP"). If your planner is a Registered Investment Advisor and a registered representative with the National Association of Securities Dealers ("NASD"), his or her activities are monitored by the Securities and Exchange Commission ("SEC") and the National Association of Securities Dealers ("NASD"). Those wishing to develop a comprehensive financial plan, should strongly consider using a planner who holds a CFP designation or RIA designation.

Questions You Should Ask

Before making a decision to engage a financial advisor, you should question them concerning their qualifications, the planning process they use, and other details of how the client-advisor relationship would work. The choice of an advisor is important and should be given the time and attention it merits. The following are some of the most important questions to ask, to help you determine if an individual is qualified.

• **Are you a Certified Financial Planner (CFP) or RIA in good standing with the SEC and NASD, and/or the Financial Planning Association ("FPA")?**
If not, ask if the advisor is enrolled in a program working toward any of those designations, or if his or her work is reviewed by someone who has any of those designations.

• **How long have you, and your firm, been in business?**
Inquire about any previous occupations and, if applicable, why the advisor changed careers.

• **What is your specific area of expertise?**
In addition, ask if the advisor's firm has a broad range of experts who can be called in to assist on your account. Find out the specialties of these in-house experts. Ideally, a large firm should have a full-time, in-house staff, representing a broad range of financial-planning disciplines, including taxation, accounting, insurance, investments, tax shelters, money management, estate planning, and retirement planning. Small firms can achieve a similar result by referring you to other professionals with whom they have working arrangements.

• **Who will be handling my account?**
If an associate will be handling your account, ask to meet that person. Be sure you interview the associate and find out his or her specialties and qualifications, including experience, licenses, and designations. Will you be able to continue to use your own accountant and lawyer? Having a good financial advisor forms a good foundation, but there are also other advisors that may be required from time to time.

• **Does your firm rely on brokerage reports and mutual fund company presentations when recommending investments, or does the firm do its own research?**
It's important to know how investment recommendations are developed.

• **Do you sell only your firm's products and services, or do you offer the best from a variety of suppliers?**
An argument could be made that if the advisor is restricted to products that are proprietary to one firm that total objectivity would be difficult.

• **How soon, and at what intervals, will I get a report or statement? What will be the scope of the report, and how personalized will it be?**
Also ask whether the firm offers newsletters or other means of educating its clients.

• **What do your services cost, and how can I be assured that I'll get my money's worth?**
There should be a definitive means of articulating what it will cost for the services that the advisor will provide. (Refer to the section which follows, entitled "How Are Financial Advisors Paid?") And, it's certainly worth finding out what to do if you are unsatisfied.

• **May I have references from clients with situations similar to mine?**
References are an invaluable way of assessing the level of satisfaction that others have experienced from the advisor's services.

• **Will I be given a written engagement letter that documents the nature and scope of the services you will provide?**
Without a written engagement agreement, walk away.

How Are Financial Advisors Paid?

The costs of developing your plan, will depend on the type and level of advice you require, and how you choose to pay for it. For example, you may require a financial advisor to make investment recommendations or address your insurance needs, or you may require your advisor to develop a comprehensive plan, that not only addresses investment and insurance advice, but also includes cash flow projections, tax strategies, retirement analysis, and estate planning. Keep in mind that a financial advisor is compensated for helping you make good decisions, not just select financial products. The right advisor will save you time and money in the long run, and also eliminate the anxiety you might face by endeavouring to handle things on your own.

Financial advisors are paid in a number of different ways. What follows is a description of three of the more common methods of compensation, each with its own merits. The most important issue is to make certain that the method of payment for any planning services is clearly outlined in writing.

Fee-Only Financial Planners

Fee-only financial planners charge exclusively for their time, much like lawyers and CPAs. These planners may charge a percentage (usually 1% to 1.5%) of assets under management, or a flat, or hourly rate. The hourly rate charged by a fee-only financial planner, can range from $50 an hour, to $350 an hour, depending on the planner's expertise and experience. Fee-only financial planners may provide you with an asset allocation, or general investment strategy, but probably won't advise you on specific investments. Implementation may be outside the mandate of the fee-only planner and is up to you, however, the planner might refer you to someone who could manage it for you.

Norm and Nancy had done a noteworthy job of managing their current affairs, but knew they needed the advice and recommendations of a financial advisor to take them to the next level. They had always maximized their IRA contributions, they both had insurance coverage, and they'd recently completed their wills and Powers of Attorney. Norm knew they had a lot of the key components already in place, but didn't know whether those components were sufficient. Had they generated enough savings to retire? Could they retire at the age they wanted to? What kind of lifestyle would their savings provide? Did they have enough insurance to support an adequate lifestyle for the survivor or did they have too much insurance? Did their wills and Powers of Attorney cover all the necessary financial aspects? As they weren't sure, Nancy scheduled a consultation with Gwen, a fee-based financial planner, to discuss their situation.

After gathering all the facts and required documents, Gwen presented a quote to prepare a comprehensive financial plan. The quote established that, in order to have their plan completed, Norm and Nancy would have to pay a monthly retainer of approximately $210. Although both Norm and Nancy thought this a reasonable amount for the required work, they stated that they couldn't afford another monthly payment because they currently had no cash surplus at month end.

Gwen demonstrated that, by simply swapping their non-deductible debt for a tax-deductible debt, they'd lower their loan repayments and reduce their taxes. By doing this, they could add a cash-flow surplus of approximately $9,000 per year, more than enough to cover their annual planning fee. She added that this was only the first strategy and that it was highly likely that their cash-flow surplus would increase further, with additional investment planning and tax strategies.

Commission-Based Financial Planners

Commission-based financial planners are typically insurance agents, mutual fund brokers, or bank employees, and they don't charge for financial planning per se. Commission-based financial planners recover their planning fee by selling financial products. Their advice in most areas is usually good, but at times, it may be more focused in areas that will involve one or more of the products they sell. Their services are useful if accumulating and protecting your assets or acquiring insurance are your major concerns.

Wayne and Yvonne were in their early 60s and wanted to set aside some money to ensure their grandchildren could afford to attend a university of their choice. Wayne and Yvonne met with a commission-based financial planner, to discuss their options. The planner suggested they direct monthly savings into a College Savings Account (529 Plan). The plan would continue to grow, tax free, and will come out tax free when used for educational purposes under current law.

Fee-Based Financial Planners

Fee-based financial planners charge fees, but may also receive commissions. The advantage is that their advice is comprehensive (like that of fee-only financial planners). They also make specific investment recommendations as required, and generally provide advice and product solutions in all necessary areas; cash and tax, risk management, and estate planning. Their fees normally range from $1,000 to $5,000 for drafting an initial plan, and in most situations, they charge an ongoing monthly retainer to provide continuous service. However, the net fee will tend to be considerably lower than that of fee-only planners, as they offset their compensation with commissions derived from helping you acquire products necessary to implement your financial plan. The net result, is that someone with a large enough asset base, may actually incur no out-of-pocket cost for the preparation of a financial plan. Typically, a fee-based financial planner will continue to work with you, to ensure your plan is implemented, monitored, updated, and adjusted as circumstances dictate.

Melinda and Nathan were in their late 50s and approaching retirement. They were very successful farmers. They'd generated significant capital through the sale of land that had been in the family for nearly 50 years. They had three children, who'd completed university and were now established in their desired careers. The fourth child remained on the farm, in hopes of establishing a farming career with his father. Both Melinda and Nathan felt reasonably secure about their future and hadn't given much thought to estate planning and possible farm-transfer scenarios, until Nathan had a heart attack that left him unable to return to his farming duties for quite some time. After this occurrence, Melinda suggested that they see a financial planner to discuss their situation.

Nathan wasn't enthusiastic. He'd always solved his own problems and always met the needs of his family. He didn't like the idea of having to pay someone a fee to come up with a strategy to eventually transfer the farm to his child. Reluctantly, Nathan went along with Melinda. They had Sam, a fee-based financial planner, meet them at their farm to discuss possible scenarios. During their conversation, it became apparent that Nathan was uneasy discussing the farm transfer because of what had occurred in his own family.

Nathan was one of three children. Since his brother and sister had gone on to pursue careers other than farming, their father had put in place a farm-transfer plan that put the farm in Nathan's name upon his father's death. This had caused a lot of bitterness between the siblings. Now, Nathan had to confront the same issue himself, and he was afraid of causing conflict among his own children.

Sam suggested that they collect additional information to try and ascertain what specifically Nathan and Melinda wanted to see happen. They scheduled a meeting with each of the children individually to determine their feelings about the situation, developed a financial plan for each of the children to become financially independent no matter what might become of the farm, and developed an estate plan to transfer the farm tax efficiently and fulfill Melinda and Nathan's wishes while maintaining family harmony. They then met with a lawyer and tax accountant to ensure strategies and agreements would pass proper tax and estate scrutiny, and finally, meet with all family members at the same time, to reveal how the estate plan would evolve and remain fair and equitable to all the children.

For Nathan, it was as if a heavy burden had been lifted from his shoulders, except he was sure this would be a troublingly expensive process. Sam informed him that, because of the compensation that would be generated from their current investment portfolio, and with the implementation of certain products after the estate plan was completed, the monthly retainer would be affordable.

Good advice shouldn't cost you; it should always pay. For example, if you pay a financial advisor $2,000 a year in fees, and they save you $2,000 in taxes, while enhancing the performance of your $300,000 portfolio by 1.5% ($4,500), then it really didn't cost $2,000. In fact, you're $4,500 ahead, and much farther ahead, when you also weigh the potential costs of not planning. The benefits of hiring a qualified financial advisor should always outweigh the costs.

Wrap Account

An investment consulting relationship in which a client's funds are placed with one or more money managers, and all administrative and management fees, along with commissions, are wrapped into one comprehensive fee, to be paid quarterly, is a wrap account. The wrap fee varies, but usually ranges from 1% to 3% of the value of the assets in the account. Wrap accounts usually require a minimum initial investment of anywhere from $25,000 to $10 million for individual accounts. The term wrap has been expanded to involve mutual fund asset allocation programs. Technically, these are not wrap programs because they are not "all inclusive." Transaction commissions in these programs on mutual funds are still a variable and they are pooled accounts as distinguished from individual accounts. From the client's point of view, a wrap account provides access to top investment managers. The financial advisor overseeing the account is paid an ongoing fee to monitor the performance of the money managers. Financial advisors may switch assets to other managers within the program if one manager consistently starts to under-perform.

Preparing to Meet Your Advisors

In creating your life and financial plans, and putting them into action, you'll likely work with professionals to help you achieve your goals.
1. A financial advisor to help develop a financial plan.
2. A financial advisor, lawyer, or trust officer to help develop an estate plan.

3. A lawyer to draft wills and/or Powers of Attorney.

4. The executor of your estate, whether a spouse, other relative, friend, or corporate executor.

To ensure that these advisors have a good understanding of your situation, you need to supply them with information of various kinds. To help you get organized to see your advisors, this planner is laid out in four sections, starting with what you'll need to see your financial advisor. Included are not only the facts you'll need to document, but also questions professional advisors will likely pose.

As you assemble this information, note that nothing is repeated, for instance, your name and personal information is only listed once. Thus, if you were meeting with your executor first, while "Your Executor(s)" is the last section, you'd need to fill out all forms first. Most people begin with a financial plan covering their retirement ("Your Financial Advisor"). Then, they incorporate an estate plan, coordinated by their financial advisor, trust officer, or lawyer; see their lawyer to draft wills and Powers of Attorney; and lastly, review everything with their executor(s).

18

Overcoming Possible Problems

Having enough income is a precondition of a satisfactory lifestyle; accumulating sufficient capital to meet all future income requirements is the definition of financial independence. Of all objectives, attaining financial independence is the most important. Your ability to fulfil this objective will depend on the strength of your financial plan. Fear of confronting the question of whether or not your accumulated capital will be sufficient to sustain your lifestyle throughout the rest of your life, can cause you to live your life less abundantly. Individuals who are already retired, fearing that they might live beyond their means and use up all their capital, may force themselves to live below their normal standards.

The way around this dilemma is to clearly identify your

spending goals, determine your present cash flow position, establish where the money will come from, face any cash-flow shortages or capital deficits head-on, and devise a strategy that will eventually limit those problems so you're able to live a worry-free life. Just because you assume that your financial resources won't be sufficient, doesn't mean that a strategy can't be devised to eliminate the problem. Not knowing where you currently stand financially, or where you're headed, will develop into a more serious problem if left to evolve on its own. Confront these issues before your situation becomes too problematic. Planning ahead for current and future problems allows you to take action prior to a crisis. If you have yet to determine how your retirement years will play out, now is the time to tackle this question.

What will you do if you discover your financial resources won't be sufficient to support your lifestyle for the remainder of your life? The answer will depend on the flexibility of your current situation. Every set of circumstances provides different opportunities and strategies. The most important aspect is determining where you're currently heading, and knowing what options you have. Below, various strategies that may be applicable to your situation are outlined. Keep in mind that each person's financial picture is unique, and there's no one solution. Nor is this a complete listing of the strategies you could use. To determine those strategies that would most effectively fit your circumstances, it's best to seek the help of a knowledgeable financial advisor.

Fear of Equities

Extensive research suggests that almost every investor, no matter how conservative his or her risk tolerance may be, should have some form of equity investments within a diversified portfolio. Yet some individuals blanch at the thought of equities. Unfortunately, their fears are heightened further by the press coverage a long bear market receives.

By contrast, people are rarely aware of the risk they take and harm they may incur by remaining 100% in fixed-income investments. For example, at time of writing, the current annual five-year fixed-income product rate is approximately 4% (January 2004). Inflation has also been running at over 2.5% on an annual basis for the last few months. So, you make 4% interest and lose 2.5% to inflation. This means that you've had a net return of 1.5%, right? If you're in the top tax bracket, you're also losing nearly half your interest earnings to taxes. Rather than getting 1.5%, you're actually down 0.5% each year; your buying power is actually shrinking, and not because you're spending it. Suppose you need a real return of 5.5% on an annual basis to live on. In that case, the buying power of your capital is decreasing by 6% per year. Here's the math: 4% return minus taxes of 2%, minus inflation of 2.5%, minus consumption of 5.5%, equals a loss in buying power of 6%. At this rate of loss, your capital will be effectively depleted in approximately 12 years.

If your fear of equities is insurmountable, what other possible solution is there that's fully guaranteed? The best solution is an annuity.

Annuities
Fixed Annuities

Annuities are one of the most widely used and reliable retirement income products in the United States. They are sold through life insurance companies and are a way to guarantee income for the rest of your life, and eliminate the fear of outliving your savings. With an annuity, you trade your capital for a lifetime pension income, one you can't outlive. Annuities are long-term vehicles, and are not considered "liquid" investments.

An annuity is a contract between you and the insurance company. You can purchase a deferred or an immediate annuity.

A **deferred annuity** is an annuity where your earnings are not taxed until you begin withdrawals. A deferred annuity may be fixed (the insurance company declares the interest rate or an index sets the annual interest rate). In addition, a deferred annuity can be classified as variable. In a deferred variable annuity you get to choose from a menu of investment options.

In an **immediate annuity** the insurance company guarantees to pay you an income for life based on your current age and life expectancy.

A **fixed annuity** provides tax-deferred growth as well as income, either for your lifetime or for a specified period of time. Fixed annuities offer a current rate of interest on premium you contribute to your policy, along with a guaranteed minimum rate for the life of the policy. Typically, the current rate is higher than the guaranteed minimum. When you buy a fixed annuity your money accumulates and compounds tax-deferred. You have several income options when you're ready to receive payments from your annuity, such as in a lump sum, over a specific period of time, or for the rest of your life.

A fixed annuity is generally a low-risk product for people who would like to know about how much they will be earning. Because you earn a fixed rate of return for a specified period, you won't have to worry about the day-to-day fluctuations of the securities markets. Annuities are not FDIC-insured, so it is important to know the financial condition of the underwriting insurance company.

Fixed annuities have two phases: the accumulation phase (when the money grows tax-deferred), and the distribution (or payout) phase. During the accumulation phase, you're basically investing money in the annuity, either through one lump sum or flexible payments over a period of time. During the distribution (or payout) phase, you withdraw your money based on the best option for you. Options include a lump sum withdrawal, in which your earnings are taxed all at once; a regular income payment schedule, which doesn't necessarily mean you won't outlive your money; or a guaranteed income plan (annuitization), in which you cannot invest any more money into your annuity, and the issuing (insurance) company begins paying you a regular income based on your contract value.

Variable Annuities ("VA")

Variable annuities provide the advantages of traditional fixed annuities with the potential returns that are available by investing your money in equity and fixed-income investments. The investment options that you may chose from in a variable annuity are referred to as "sub-accounts." These sub-accounts are structured as segregated "investment portfolios" that are managed by professional investment managers.

Many variable annuities offer more than one investment company (mutual fund company) to choose from and within each investment company you many chose from a variety of sub-accounts with different investment objectives. This allows you to diversify your portfolio to minimize risk and maximize potential investment return. Unlike fixed annuities with guaranteed protection against loss of principal, your principal is at risk and subject to loss in value.

Annuities have long been an important piece of any retirement portfolio. For years, financial professionals have praised the attributes of fixed and variable annuities as long-term savings and retirement vehicles.

Equity Index Annuities ("EIA")

In recent years, equity-index annuities have become more and more popular as an investment alternative for the individual who wants to participate in stock market returns, and yet protect their assets from market downturns.

As with fixed annuities, equity-index annuities have all the same features and guarantee of principal. The most significant difference is how the annuity's interest is credited. With a traditional fixed annuity, the interest rate credited to the contract is usually based on the prevailing market rates. With an EIA, the interest rate credited to the contract is not determined each year by the insurance company. Instead, it is based on an interest-crediting formula that is linked to an independent stock market index. The index to which most EIAs on the market today tie their interest rates is the Standard & Poor's Composite Stock Price Index (the S&P 500), which is considered a significant barometer of the performance of U. S. equity markets. Also available are Dow Jones equity-index annuities, and NASDQ equity-index annuities. Interest rates paid on an equity-index annuity will have a cap, depending on the crediting methodology. Index interest is credited on an annual basis.

An EIA provides an opportunity to achieve potentially greater growth and inflation protection, without market risk to principal. In addition, like all annuities, the EIA can be used to provide its owner a steam of income that's guaranteed to last as long as they live. This income is typically used in retirement to supplement other sources of income such as personal savings, Social Security and pension benefits.

In today's marketplace, indexing has become very popular. Studies have proven that over time the stock market has outperformed inflation and many other types of investments. The EIA is another opportunity to employ this popular strategy. EIAs are, however, very different than indexed mutual funds. Indexed mutual funds carry market risk; the risk of loss due to fluctuations in the stock market. Index annuities do not carry market risk. As discussed earlier, EIAs are fixed annuities, and as such the risk is borne by the insurance company, not the annuity owner. The annuity owner's principal is guaranteed.

Reverse Mortgages
A Mortgage Tailor-Made for Seniors

For people in retirement, there's your pension, Social Security and any savings and investments you will have built up by then. Altogether, you hope this will be enough to see you through the rest of your life. But what if it's not?

Declining interest rates have hammered the income generated from money market funds and bank CDs that many senior citizens depend on. And the bear market has pulverized investment portfolios. For many retirees, the golden years are starting to get a little green around the edges. What can you do if you aren't able to live your retirement dreams?

Many seniors continue to retain one valuable asset: their home. Well, then, perhaps you can tap the equity in your home.

Many homeowners have this in the back of their minds. At a certain age, they anticipate that they may have to sell their home and move someplace cheaper, using the difference to make ends meet.

But there's an alternative: a reverse mortgage. It's a way of taking substantial amounts of money out of your home without selling or ever having to make loan payments, as you would with a second mortgage or home equity loan. Basically, a reverse mortgage is a loan that uses the home as collateral, just as a regular mortgage does. The homeowner retains title to the home including the right to sell at any time and upon death the house passes onto his or her estate.

Retirees are spared the qualification process that is required for other types of loans. You don't need an income, good credit or other assets to qualify, as you do with most loans because you will not be making monthly loan payments; in fact repayment of the loan is entirely deferred until you permanently leave the home.

With most home loans you run the risk of losing your home to lender foreclosure if you fail to make your monthly payments. This concern is completely eliminated with a reverse mortgage because there are no monthly payments to make.

A reverse mortgage is a special type of loan available ONLY to individuals who are 62 years and older, which allows them to convert the equity in their homes into cash. Many seniors are using the money from a reverse mortgage to provide them with the financial security they need to fully enjoy their retirement years.

The reverse mortgage is aptly named because the payment stream is "reversed." Instead of making monthly payments to a lender, as with a regular first mortgage or home equity loan, a lender makes payments to you.

What makes reverse mortgages so appealing is the fact that you can enjoy unrestricted use of the money and the loan does not have to be paid back for as long as you live in your home. This provides peace of mind and gives retirees what they want and need; additional cash, not additional debt.

The money from a reverse mortgage can be used for ANYTHING: daily living expenses; home repairs and home modifications; medical bills and prescription drugs; pay-off of existing debts; travel; long-term health care; prevention of foreclosure; and other retirement and investment needs.   It may surprise you to know that you are eligible for a reverse mortgage even if you still owe money on a first or second mortgage. In fact, many seniors get a reverse mortgage specifically to pay off their burdensome mortgage debts.   Many seniors who have accumulated large credit card balances are using reverse mortgages to wipe out their outstanding credit card debt.

You can choose how to receive the money from a reverse mortgage. The options are: all at once (lump sum); fixed monthly payments (for up to life); a line of credit; or a combination of these — all without income tax or capital gains tax. The most popular option — chosen by more than 70 percent of borrowers

— is the line of credit, which allows you to draw any amount of the loan proceeds at any time you wish.

The size of the reverse mortgage that you can get depends on your age at the time you apply for the loan, the value of your home, current interest rates, and where you live. In general, the older you are and the more valuable your home (and the less you owe on your home), the larger the reverse mortgage can be.

The costs associated with getting a reverse mortgage include the origination fee (which can be financed as part of the mortgage), an appraisal fee, and other charges similar to those for regular mortgages.

The money provided to you from a reverse mortgage does not affect regular Social Security or Medicare benefits. In fact, the funds received from a properly structured reverse mortgage need not affect your eligibility for other kinds of government assistance, such as Medi-Cal, SSI or other state assistance programs.

The interest rate charged to a reverse mortgage changes every month or once a year, depending on the option chosen by the borrower. Rates go up and down according to changes in the yields of one-year U.S. Treasury notes. Historically, over the past 20 years, the average rate of the one-year U.S. Treasury note has been a little less than 6%. If history repeats itself, a reverse mortgage borrower can expect the debt on a reverse mortgage to grow at about a 7% rate over the life of the loan.

To help you evaluate whether a reverse mortgage is an appropriate option, you are required to speak either in person or over the phone to a reverse mortgage counselor who is trained to provide unbiased objective information regarding the reverse mortgage concept. Your reverse mortgage lender can arrange this meeting for you. The counselor will educate you about reverse mortgages and will discuss other alternative options that are available to you.

No payments are due on a reverse mortgage as long as you continue to live in the home. The loan becomes due and payable when you cease to occupy your home as a principal residence. This can occur if you (the last remaining spouse, in cases of couples) pass away, sell the home, or permanently move out. The repayment obligation is equal to the sum of the total funds received by the borrower, interest, and any closing costs and other charges financed as part of the loan.

The home does not have to be sold to pay off the loan. You (or your heirs) can pay off the reverse mortgage by refinancing the loan. Otherwise, the lender is repaid when the home is sold. If the sale's proceeds exceed the amount owed, excess proceeds go to the borrower or borrower's heirs/estate. If the proceeds are less than the amount owed, the lender absorbs the shortfall. In any event, the borrower's loan repayment obligation can never exceed the value of the home at the time of repayment.

The fact that the debt can never exceed the value of the home highlights the safety of the reverse mortgage concept, which is the underlying premise upon which it is built. This loan is a non-recourse loan. Simply put, it means that the only asset the lender can claim for repayment of this loan is the home. No matter how much the loan grows, no matter how many other assets the borrower or the heirs own, no matter how little value remains in the home, the lender is restricted from collecting the debt from any other asset besides the home. If the loan is greater than the home's value, it is the lenders problem, not the borrower's problem.

A reverse mortgage therefore does not saddle you or your estate with any debt beyond that which can be paid by selling the property. Once the home is sold, any money remaining after the debt is paid goes to the homeowner or heirs. One of the chief misconceptions about these loans is that the lender gets the home when the owner dies.

Reverse mortgages with a debt that is growing is much riskier for lenders than other mortgages on which the debt is systematically reduced by monthly payments. Why would a lender accept these loan terms and willingly make loans that are so heavily weighted in the borrower's favor? How could a lender assume the risk of waiting so long to be repaid with no guarantee that home which is the underlying asset will have sufficient value to repay the full loan amount?

To induce lending institutions to make these loans to retirees, the US Government agreed to protect lenders against the possible consequences of this unprotected arrangement; thus, the creation of the HUD/FHA reverse mortgage loan program that today accounts for 90% of all the reverse mortgages created in the US.

The FHA Home Equity Conversion Mortgage (HECM) is the oldest and most popular reverse mortgage product. Available since 1989 to homeowners 62 or older, HECMs are insured by the federal government through the Federal Housing Administration (FHA), a part of the US Department of Housing and Urban Development. HUD's guarantee to lenders stipulates that in the event that the home value is not sufficient to repay the full value of the loan, HUD will make up the shortfall to the lender.

The size of a HECM varies with: (1) the borrower's age; (2) the value of the home; and (3) current interest rates. The location of your home also affects the loan size. The maximum size of a HECM depends on the FHA loan limit, which varies from area to area and is usually adjusted annually.

Currently (for 2004), the FHA loan limit for the majority of Southern California counties is $290,319, but the actual loan amount available to any borrower is a percentage of this figure. The percentage is based on a formula that takes into consideration two factors; the borrowers' ages and the prevailing interest rates. Older borrowers receive a higher percentage of the FHA loan limit than do younger borrowers. Lower interest rates allow for a higher percentage of the FHA loan limit, hence all borrowers benefit from today's low interest rate environment.

Consider, for example, the amount that might be borrowed through an HECM loan on a debt-free $300,000 home in Southern California. A 66 year old homeowner could be allowed to borrow up to $166,000, while a 74 year old could get $185,000, and an 85 year old could get $215,000.

Since the maximum loan amount is set when the loan is granted and is based on interest rates at that time, it's worth looking at reverse mortgages now. By getting a loan while rates are low, you can lock in the larger loan amount. That figure will stay the same even though the interest rate will be adjusted in the future.

The HUD/FHA loan provides very significant safety features to the borrower as well. The FHA loan is strictly regulated and monitored by HUD to eliminate the possibility of any unfair lending practices or excessive lender charges. HUD has created a system of checks and balances that make it next to impossible for any abuses to take place. The rules, regulations, loan terms, interest rates and loan fees are absolutely dictated by HUD, and rigorously enforced to allow no room for any type of lender deviation. The lending activity of FHA lenders is carefully scrutinized and regularly audited to protect borrowers against any form of abuse.

Typically, the only out-of-pocket cost that a borrower must pay for upfront is the appraisal fee. Appraisal fees generally range between $375 and $450. The remaining closing costs and fees are usually financed as part of the reverse mortgage.

While reverse mortgages have been around for decades, their popularity in the past few years has soared to record levels as more and more seniors are integrating reverse mortgages into their overall retirement planning as a supplement to their income or to increase their cash reserves.

With today's low interest rates and highly appreciated home values, reverse mortgages are certainly worth a look. When rates are low, you can get more money out of your home, and there is likely to be more value left in the property when you sell or pass it to your heirs.

Financial Independence Deficit

Financial independence means you've accumulated enough financial resources to sufficiently meet all future income requirements.

What happens if your current investment capital and revenue sources don't meet your lifestyle expenditures, and the outcome indicates you'll run out of money? Three things can alter this situation:

1. Increase your current investment return.
2. Decrease your current lifestyle expenditures.
3. Increase your current investment return, while simultaneously reducing your current lifestyle expenditures.

In addition, various strategies can reduce current taxation, which in turn will increase annual cash flow, new cash management ideas can reduce your current living expenditures by changing your spending habits, and revised investment strategies may be more tax-efficient, and provide a higher long-term after-tax annual return on your investments.

Remember that forging ahead without a strategy increases your likelihood of failing to meet your needs. There are many knowledgeable financial advisors who can work closely with you to provide sensible solutions to help reduce any deficit you face. Deciding what happens today, will determine what happens tomorrow. If you decide to work with an advisor to develop strategies to help you overcome any shortages, your chances of success increase. And having the courage to confront a crisis before it happens, enhances your probability of avoiding that crisis. Many strategies, outside those described in this book, can help you achieve peace of mind by knowing you'll be okay in the future, but the first step, the decision to act, is up to you.

Family Dynamics

Although this book was not designed to explore all the family dynamics that can occur when a parent must become dependent on his or her adult children, one of its goals is to encourage both adult children and parents to prepare financially for the ramifications of aging, to discuss the possibility that parent dependence might occur and confront the issues prior to experiencing a crisis.

People are often peculiar when it comes to allowing others access to their financial information, even when that other person is a family member. Some individuals value their independence so highly, that they'd rather suffer than ask for help. If you're one of these, know that, by addressing the issue, no matter how independent you are or however embarrassing your situation, you'll make life easier for both yourself and your adult children.

Pearl and Ed, both in their late 70s, were struggling financially. They couldn't bring themselves to ask their son, Marty, for his help. He had his own family to look after and, they felt, they would just be a burden on him. Eventually, it got so bad, they had no choice. They were running out money and had no other options to supplement their monthly income.

They considered selling their home, but didn't want to do this. They loved their home and it was big enough for their grandkids to come and spend weekends with them. They enjoyed these times so much. Besides, how long would the money from their home sale really last? Ed and Pearl realized that, if they put their home up for sale, they'd have to tell their son the reason. But he was going to find out eventually. They might as well speak with him now.

One day, when Marty came over to drop their

grandchildren off for the weekend, they mustered the strength to speak with him. He was more than happy to help out as much as he could. They were his parents, who'd taken care of him for so many years, and both were a true blessing to him. He never hesitated to return the favour. Marty suggested that his parents, he and his wife, go and see his financial advisor as soon as possible, to determine what type of help Pearl and Ed needed, and how much help could be provided.

Adult children and parents should be encouraged to talk to each other. Inquiring about your parents' financial status is a sign of caring, and not invasion. In fact, given the nation's aging population, if you're a baby boomer, planning together with elderly parents is a prerequisite for your own successful financial future.

Appendix A
Types of Insurance

Disability Insurance

Short-Term Disability

Short-term disability, sometimes called weekly indemnity, is normally provided under an employee group benefit plan. Typically it'll have a starting date ranging from 0 to 15 days following the disability. Benefits usually extend from 15 to 52 weeks and provide two-thirds of the employee's basic weekly income.

Long-Term Disability

Long-term disability may be provided either through your employer or must be purchased through a personal policy. Benefits for long-term disability under an employee group plan almost always begin when the short-term disability benefits end. Thus, if the short-term disability has a benefits duration of

15 weeks, the long-term disability plan will usually commence benefits after 15 weeks. The benefits duration of long-term disability group plans is usually to age 65.

Under personal policies, the start dates can vary from 31 days to 365 days.

Critical Illness Disability

Critical illness protection is a benefit payable if the insured is diagnosed with one of a number of covered illnesses: Alzheimer's, benign brain tumor, blindness, cancer, coma, coronary artery bypass surgery, deafness, heart attack, kidney failure, loss of limbs, loss of speech, major organ transplant, multiple sclerosis, occupational HIV, paralysis, Parkinson's, severe burns, stroke, and others. Unlike a monthly disability benefit, which is designed to replace income, this type of benefit pays a lump sum in the event of a critical illness.

Some of the benefits that can be included in a critical illness policy are: return of premium on death (if you die and haven't claimed a benefit, premiums paid for the coverage will be returned), return of premium on expiry (if coverage expires and you haven't made a claim, you receive your premiums back), and functional independence rider (if you suffer an unlisted severe disability or illness, and the illness affects your personal independence, you may receive a monthly benefit to aid in the expense of receiving assistance).

The different terms available under critical illness insurance are to age 65, to age 75, and even life coverage. The premiums will vary depending on your health, age, and the term selected.

Long-Term Care

Long-term care insurance allows more control over your lifestyle, independence, health, and finances. It allows you to choose where to go, versus being told where to go.

Long-term care insurance covers care expenses in your own

home, or in a facility of your choosing. The periods range from a couple years to life, depending on the benefit selected. You can receive anywhere from $50 to $300 per day.

When you begin receiving benefits, your premiums will cease. The payment period (the amount of time you have to continue paying premiums) is normally limited, depending on your current age. Although the insurance company will check your medical history, there's normally no medical examination, other than a telephone interview.

Life Insurance

Some forms of life insurance, known as term insurance, protect you for a specific period of time. Others, such as Term to 100, Universal Life and Whole Life, offer permanent protection.

Term Insurance

Term insurance is life insurance purchased at a cost or premium for a specified time period (1 year, 5 years, 10 years, 15 years, 20 years, to age 65, etc.). It's insurance in its purest form. There's normally no cash surrender value should the policy be cancelled.

When you need a specific amount of coverage for a specific amount of time, and your cash flow is limited, term insurance is a good choice. If you anticipate an improvement in your cash flow, term insurance can be acquired with an option to convert to permanent life insurance (Term to 100, Universal, or Whole Life) at a later date. Be sure to choose a quality insurance company that offers products allowing conversion from term insurance into permanent insurance.

To determine the most cost effective type of term insurance, you need to analyze the total cost of various plans over the time the insurance is required. Be sure the plan you select is renewable at guaranteed rates and includes a disability waiver of premium if you're currently working.

Term to 100

Term to 100 is the simplest form of permanent insurance. It's available for the whole life of the policyholder. Term to 100 provides a set amount of coverage with level premiums. In some cases, premiums will be payable for life; in others, the payment period might be reduced to 20 years, or age 65.

If you have a long-term, continuing need for life insurance, and limited cash flow, Term to 100 should be acquired. Features of the plan should include guaranteed rates and a disability waiver of premium in the event that you're still working.

Universal Life

Universal life is a flexible type of permanent insurance. The amount of coverage can be changed in the event of changes in your circumstances, subject to various contractual limitations. Premiums or deposits can also be adjusted as your cash flow changes, although minimum and maximum premiums do apply.

Deposits can normally be made in excess of the actual cost of the insurance. These excess deposits are invested within the policy, attracting no tax on interest earnings while the funds remain in the policy. The tax act provides guidelines on the maximum tax-exempt value that can accrue in the policy. All insurance companies monitor these amounts on behalf of their policyholders to make certain that the policies stay tax-exempt.

Investment options for surplus cash invested within the policy vary with each insurance company, but should include a variety of deposit terms, mutual funds, and indexed funds.

Universal life should be considered when coverage is required, or desired, beyond retirement, and when there is a cash-flow surplus.

Whole Life

Whole life insurance is normally less flexible than universal life. There are many variations of whole life.

In participating whole life, the policyholder participates in the upside of a company's ability to manage its reserves through the payment of dividends.

Premiums for this type of insurance are always greater in the early years than the actual cost of the insurance. The degree to which the premium exceeds the actual cost of insurance will determine the long-term cash accumulation that occurs within the policy. Usually, the higher the premium, the higher the cash value accumulation.

The long-term performance of this type of insurance depends on the results the insurance company achieves, relative to its death claims and operating expenses. The greatest factor governing performance of a whole life policy, is the investment returns on the surplus premiums that the company achieves. Any excess premiums collected by the insurance company are refunded to the policyholder in the form of a dividend, which can be received in cash, or reinvested to increase the death benefits and/or cash value of the policy.

Funds accumulating in the whole life policy are not subject to taxation, provided the policy falls within the guidelines of IRC Section 7702A(a)(1).

Whole life should be used when there's a permanent need for coverage beyond retirement, and cash flow is flexible.

Appendix B

Preparing to Meet Your Advisors

Your Financial Advisor

What follows is the basic information you should assemble before meeting with your advisor to create a financial plan, including retirement, or, if you're already retired, a retirement income plan.

About You

Full name: _____

Telephone: _____

Address: _____

_____

Date of birth: _____

Place of birth: _____

Location of birth certificate: _____

Citizenship papers: ☐ yes ☐ no

Location: _____

Social Insurance/Social Security #: _____

Health impairments (if any): _____

_____

Health insurance #: _____

Driver's license #: _____

Occupation: _____

Employer: _____

Marital Status

☐ Single ☐ Married ☐ Common Law ☐ Separated

☐ Divorced ☐ Widowed

☐ Marriage certificate   Date: _____

☐ Prenuptial agreement   Date: _____

☐ Domestic agreement   Date: _____

☐ Separation agreement   Date: _____

☐ Divorce judgement   Date: _____

Location of document(s): _____

(Your advisor or lawyer will want to see these documents when your estate plan is drafted.)

Military service: ☐ yes ☐ no

Country served: _____

Veteran's number: _____

Location of discharge papers: _____

(Only your executor needs this military information.)

Spouse or Partner

Complete this section for your current spouse or partner, and also any former spouse(s), if relevant.

Full name: _____

Telephone: _____

Address: _____

_____

Date of birth: _____

Place of birth: _____

Location of birth certificate: _____

Citizenship papers: ☐ yes ☐ no

Location: _____

Social Insurance/Social Security #: _____

Health impairments (if any): _____

_____

Health insurance #: _____

Driver's license #: _____

Occupation: _____

Employer: _____

Marital Status

☐ Single ☐ Married ☐ Common Law ☐ Separated
☐ Divorced ☐ Widowed

☐ Marriage certificate Date: _____
☐ Prenuptial agreement Date: _____
☐ Domestic agreement Date: _____
☐ Separation agreement Date: _____
☐ Divorce judgement Date: _____
Location of document(s): _____

(Your advisor or lawyer will want to see these documents when your estate plan is drafted.)

Military service: ☐ yes ☐ no
Country served: _____
Veteran's number: _____
Location of discharge papers: _____
(Only your executor needs this military information.)

Children

Complete this information for each child.

Child of: _____
Full name: _____
Date of birth: _____
Age to receive benefits from my estate: _____

If independent:
Telephone: _____
Address: _____

☐ Single ☐ Married ☐ Common Law ☐ Separated
☐ Divorced ☐ Widowed

If dependent (lawyer and executor will need to know):
Full name of guardian named in will: _____
Relationship to my child and me: _____
Telephone: _____
Address: _____
_____

Alternate guardian: _____
Relationship to my child and me: _____
Telephone: _____
Address: _____
_____

Child of: _____
Full name: _____
Date of birth: _____
Age to receive benefits from my estate: _____

If independent:
Telephone: _____
Address: _____
_____

☐ Single ☐ Married ☐ Common Law ☐ Separated
☐ Divorced ☐ Widowed

If dependent (lawyer and executor will need to know):
Full name of guardian named in will: _____
Relationship to my child and me: _____
Telephone: _____
Address: _____
_____

Alternate guardian: _____
Relationship to my child and me: _____
Telephone: _____
Address: _____
_____

Child of: _____

Full name: _____

Date of birth: _____

Age to receive benefits from my estate: _____

If independent:

Telephone: _____

Address: _____

☐ Single ☐ Married ☐ Common Law ☐ Separated
☐ Divorced ☐ Widowed

If dependent (lawyer and executor will need to know):

Full name of guardian named in will: _____

Relationship to my child and me: _____

Telephone: _____

Address: _____

Alternate guardian: _____

Relationship to my child and me: _____

Telephone: _____

Address: _____

Parents

Complete this information for each of your parents still living, and each parent of your spouse or partner still living.

Parent of: _____
Full name: _____
Date of birth: _____
Address: _____

Health impairments (if any): _____

Financial status: ☐ Dependent   ☐ Independent
                        ☐ Will likely leave an inheritance

Parent of: _____
Full name: _____
Date of birth: _____
Address: _____

Health impairments (if any): _____

Financial status: ☐ Dependent   ☐ Independent
                        ☐ Will likely leave an inheritance

Parent of: _____
Full name: _____
Date of birth: _____
Address: _____

Health impairments (if any): _____

Financial status: ☐ Dependent   ☐ Independent
                        ☐ Will likely leave an inheritance

Parent of: _____

Full name: _____

Date of birth: _____

Address: _____

_____

Health impairments (if any): _____

_____

Financial status: ☐ Dependent ☐ Independent
                   ☐ Will likely leave an inheritance

Bank Accounts

Be sure to list all bank accounts, so your executor or family can find the money in these accounts.

Name on account: _____

Bank: _____

Branch: _____

Account #: _____

☐ Savings ☐ Checking

Name on account: _____

Bank: _____

Branch: _____

Account #: _____

☐ Savings ☐ Checking

Name on account: _____

Bank: _____

Branch: _____

Account #: _____

☐ Savings ☐ Checking

Documents/Information

Provide this information for your spouse or partner (if any), as well.

☐ Last three payroll stubs (if employed)
☐ Employee Benefits booklet(s) (unless retired)
☐ Most recent Employee Benefits statement(s) (unless retired)
☐ Most recent Pension Plan statement(s) and/or Plan booklets (unless retired)
☐ Last two years' personal Income Tax returns
☐ Most current financial statements (for all corporate, proprietor, or partnership interests)
☐ Details of any investments or real estate
☐ Social Security Statement of Contributions (if you have one)
☐ IRAs Individual Retirement Accounts both Traditional/Roth (most recent statements)
☐ CDs Certificates of Deposit (most recent statements)
☐ Stock portfolio (most recent statements)
☐ Mutual funds (most recent statements)
☐ Annuities (copy of contract)
☐ Mortgages receivable (money that is owed to you)
☐ Limited Partnership Offering memorandum, Executive Summary, and most current correspondence
☐ Documentation for all current liabilities (mortgages, lines of credit, credit card statements, etc.)
☐ Life, Disability, Critical Illness, and Long-term Care insurance policies
☐ Shareholder's/business agreements (if applicable)
☐ Family Trust documentation (if applicable)

Financial Independence

Ideally, at some point, you'll have enough income from pensions, government benefits, and/or personal investments, not to need employment income to maintain your lifestyle (i.e., you can retire comfortably).

If you're not already financially independent, at what age, realistically, would you like to be financially independent?

Age: _____

If you're already retired, what amount of annual net-after-tax income do you require each year to maintain your chosen lifestyle?

$ _____

If you're not already retired, what amount of net-after-tax annual income would you want during your retirement years?

$ _____

Capital Outlay

List major items you'll need money for, over the next few years, that aren't part of your regular budget (e.g., cars, home upgrades, cottage, etc.).

Item	Dollars Needed	Year Required	Savings on Hand
_____	$_____	_____	$_____
Item	Dollars Needed	Year Required	Savings on Hand
_____	$_____	_____	$_____
Item	Dollars Needed	Year Required	Savings on Hand
_____	$_____	_____	$_____
Item	Dollars Needed	Year Required	Savings on Hand
_____	$_____	_____	$_____

Educational Outlay

Specify all educational costs you'll need to fund.

Child/Grandchild	Age	Amount Required	# of Years	Plan in Place
_____	____	$_____	_____	☐ yes ☐ no
Child/Grandchild	Age	Amount Required	# of Years	Plan in Place
_____	____	$_____	_____	☐ yes ☐ no
Child/Grandchild	Age	Amount Required	# of Years	Plan in Place
_____	____	$_____	_____	☐ yes ☐ no
Child/Grandchild	Age	Amount Required	# of Years	Plan in Place
_____	____	$_____	_____	☐ yes ☐ no
Child/Grandchild	Age	Amount Required	# of Years	Plan in Place
_____	____	$_____	_____	☐ yes ☐ no

Risk Management

In the event of my death, my family would need $_____/year.
If I'm disabled, my family would need $_____/year.

Estate

The following best describes my/our estate objectives:
☐ Maximize what I/we have for my/our personal benefit (e.g., spend my/our last dollar on the day I/we die); or
☐ Live comfortably, be secure in the future, and maximize the balance of my/our estate for the benefit of children, and grandchildren; or
☐ Maximize the value of my/our charitable donations and/or bequests, without impacting my/our financial security.
☐ Other (specify): _____

Savings

Currently I/we are saving the following:

IRAs: $ _____ per ☐ month ☐ year
Current Total $ _____

Education Savings: $ _____ per ☐ month ☐ year
Current Total $ _____

Other (specify): _____
$ _____ per ☐ month ☐ year
Current Total $ _____

Priorities

Rank your priorities, with #1 being most important, #2 being less important, etc. Note: You can only have one #1. Put N/A opposite any items that are not applicable to you.

My/Our Priorities (Not Retired)	Me	Partner/ Spouse
Education Savings for children/grandchildren	_____	_____
Saving to retire early	_____	_____
Saving to have more retirement income	_____	_____
Paying off debts (including mortgage)	_____	_____
Enhancing my/our lifestyle now (home upgrade, cottage, new car, etc.)	_____	_____
Knowing the family is protected in the event of death or disability	_____	_____
Helping parents	_____	_____
Other (specify): _____	_____	_____

My/Our Priorities (Retired)	Me	Partner/ Spouse
Education Savings for children/grandchildren	_____	_____
Increasing my/our income to spend more now	_____	_____

Leaving an estate to my/our children   _____ _____

Capital spending (home upgrade,
world travel, new car, etc.)   _____ _____

Money to charities   _____ _____

Making sure my/our income lasts longer
than I/we do   _____ _____

Other (specify): _____   _____ _____

Your Estate-Planning Advisor

The following checklists will help you judge your state of readiness to see your lawyer to draft or update wills or Powers of Attorney. Don't procrastinate about seeing an advisor until you can say yes to everything on these lists, or you likely will never have an estate plan. Your advisor will work with you to complete them.

Setting your estate planning priorities	Yes	No	Not Sure
I know how I want my assets to be distributed.	☐	☐	☐
There will be sufficient assets to satisfy the charitable and other gifts I have in mind.	☐	☐	☐
There will be a source of income for my family when I die.	☐	☐	☐
There will be a source of income if I'm disabled.	☐	☐	☐
I know what my income will be at retirement.	☐	☐	☐
My estate is reasonably creditor-proof.	☐	☐	☐
I know what the tax exposure is in my estate.	☐	☐	☐
I know how any taxes will be paid.	☐	☐	☐

Taking an inventory of your estate	Yes	No	Not Sure
All my important papers are together.	☐	☐	☐
My executor knows where they are.	☐	☐	☐
I have a will.	☐	☐	☐
I know my will is up to date.	☐	☐	☐
I have a current net-worth statement.	☐	☐	☐
I know what will be left in my estate after paying all my debts and distributing specified gifts and legacies.	☐	☐	☐

Executors, guardians, agents

	Yes	No	Not Sure
I have chosen my executor(s).	☐	☐	☐
He or she or they know of my choice.	☐	☐	☐
I have explained my expectations to him/her/them.	☐	☐	☐
I have chosen alternate executors.	☐	☐	☐
I have chosen a guardian(s) for each child.	☐	☐	☐
He or she or they know of my choice.	☐	☐	☐
I have explained my expectations to him/her/them.	☐	☐	☐
I have chosen alternate guardians.	☐	☐	☐
I have appointed an agent for property.	☐	☐	☐
He or she or they know of my choice.	☐	☐	☐
I have explained my expectations to him/her/them.	☐	☐	☐
I have appointed an agent for personal care.	☐	☐	☐
He or she or they know of my choice.	☐	☐	☐
I have explained my expectations to him/her/them.	☐	☐	☐

Your family

	Yes	No	Not Sure
I have made funeral plans.	☐	☐	☐
I have discussed them with my family.	☐	☐	☐
I have had a family meeting to talk about my estate plan and the provisions of my will.	☐	☐	☐
My family has met my professional advisors.	☐	☐	☐
My family knows who I've appointed as my executor(s).	☐	☐	☐
My family has met my executor(s).	☐	☐	☐
My family knows who I've appointed as my children's guardian(s).	☐	☐	☐
My family has met my children's guardian(s).	☐	☐	☐
My life insurance beneficiary information is up to date.	☐	☐	☐

My family knows who I've appointed as my
agents for property and personal care. □ □ □

My family has met my agents for property
and personal care. □ □ □

Gifts

To ensure there are sufficient assets to meet your estate requirements, you'll need to address the following.

Money

Include charitable gifts.

Amount: $ _____

Full name of beneficiary: _____

Relationship to me: _____

Telephone: _____

Address: _____

_____

Restrictions (if any): _____

Amount: $ _____

Full name of beneficiary: _____

Relationship to me: _____

Telephone: _____

Address: _____

_____

Restrictions (if any): _____

Specific Assets

Description of assets: _____

Full name of beneficiary: _____

Relationship to me: _____

Telephone: _____

Address: _____

_____

Restrictions (if any): _____

Description of assets: _____
Full name of beneficiary: _____
Relationship to me: _____
Telephone: _____
Address: _____

_____
Restrictions (if any): _____

Residual Beneficiaries

The residue is what will be left in your estate, after paying your debts and distributing specific gifts and legacies. It's recommended that the residue be divided among beneficiaries by percentage.

Full name: _____
Relationship to me: _____
Telephone: _____
Address: _____

_____
Proportion of residue to be allotted: _____%

Full name: _____
Relationship to me: _____
Telephone: _____
Address: _____

_____
Proportion of residue to be allotted: _____%

Full name: _____
Relationship to me: _____
Telephone: _____
Address: _____

_____
Proportion of residue to be allotted: _____%

Full name: _____

Relationship to me: _____

Telephone: _____

Address: _____

_____

Proportion of residue to be allotted: _____%

Valuables

Include antiques, collectibles, fine art, etc. of substantial value.

Description: _____

Appraised value: _____

Insured against loss or damage: ☐ yes ☐ no

Description: _____

Appraised value: _____

Insured against loss or damage: ☐ yes ☐ no

Description: _____

Appraised value: _____

Insured against loss or damage: ☐ yes ☐ no

Description: _____

Appraised value: _____

Insured against loss or damage: ☐ yes ☐ no

Your Lawyer

In addition, your lawyer will need the following information.

Executor(s)

Complete for each executor and all alternates.

Full name: _____
☐ Executor ☐ Alternate
Relationship to me: _____
Telephone: _____
Address: _____

_____

Full name: _____
☐ Executor ☐ Alternate
Relationship to me: _____
Telephone: _____
Address: _____

_____

Will

I have made a will. ☐ yes ☐ no
Location of original: _____
Location of copy: _____
Date of will or last update: _____
I have made a "living will." ☐ yes ☐ no
Location: _____

I wish to donate my organs or body for transplant, medical research, or education. ☐ yes ☐ no
This is explained:
☐ in my will
☐ on my driver's license
☐ on an organ donor card Location: _____

Instructions for the distribution of my personal effects are provided in my will. ☐ yes ☐ no

Powers of Attorney

Complete for each agent and all alternates.

Full name: _____
☐ Agent ☐ Alternate
For: ☐ Property ☐ Personal care ☐ Other
Relationship to you: _____
Telephone: _____
Address: _____

Location of document: _____

Full name: _____
☐ Agent ☐ Alternate
For: ☐ Property ☐ Personal care ☐ Other
Relationship to you: _____
Telephone: _____
Address: _____

Location of document: _____

Full name: _____
☐ Agent ☐ Alternate
For: ☐ Property ☐ Personal care ☐ Other
Relationship to you: _____
Telephone: _____
Address: _____

Location of document: _____

Full name: _____

☐ Agent ☐ Alternate

For: ☐ Property ☐ Personal care ☐ Other

Relationship to you: _____

Telephone: _____

Address: _____

_____

Location of document: _____

Funeral Arrangements

Consider a pre-planned funeral.

I have made funeral arrangements. ☐ yes ☐ no

Funeral home: _____

Telephone: _____

Address: _____

_____

I have set out instructions for burial/cremation or funeral.

☐ yes ☐ no

These instructions are:

☐ in my will

☐ in a letter Location: _____

I own a cemetery plot. ☐ yes ☐ no

Location of plot: _____

Location of deed: _____

I have provided for the ongoing care of my plot. ☐ yes ☐ no

Your Executor

Additional information you should provide to your executor.

Important Contacts

Include your employer/business office, lawyer(s), accountant, financial advisor, bank manager, doctor, and, even dentist.

Name: _____

Relationship to me: _____

Telephone: _____

Address: _____

_____

Name: _____

Relationship to me: _____

Telephone: _____

Address: _____

_____

Name: _____

Relationship to me: _____

Telephone: _____

Address: _____

_____

Safety Deposit Box

I have a safety deposit box. ☐ yes ☐ no

Location: _____

Names of others who have access to it: _____

Location of keys: _____

Location of list of contents: _____

Vehicles

Include cars, boats, etc.

Description: _____

License #: _____

Location of ownership documents: _____

Appendix C
Interviewing a Financial Advisor

The following are key questions to ask a financial advisor before making a decision to work with that advisor:

1. What is your educational background?

College degree: ☐ yes _____ ☐ no
Area of study: _____

Graduate degree: ☐ yes _____ ☐ no
Area of study: _____

Financial Planning education and designations:
☐ Certified Financial Planner
☐ Registered Investment Advisor
☐ Accountant
☐ Other: _____

2. Do you have experience in providing advice on the following topics?

Retirement planning:	☐ yes	☐ no
Cash management:	☐ yes	☐ no
Investment planning:	☐ yes	☐ no
Tax planning:	☐ yes	☐ no
Estate planning:	☐ yes	☐ no
Insurance planning:	☐ yes	☐ no
Intergenerational planning:	☐ yes	☐ no

Other: _____

3. How long have you been offering financial planning advice?
☐ Less than 2 years
☐ 2–5 years
☐ More than 5 years
☐ More than 10 years

4. What are your areas of specialization, and what qualifies you in this field?

_____

_____

5. What continuing education in financial planning do you pursue?
☐ 1–14 hours of professional education each year
☐ 15–30 hours of professional education each year
☐ More than 30 hours of professional education each year

6. What licenses do you hold?
☐ Mutual Funds
☐ Securities
☐ Insurance
☐ Other: _____

7. Have you ever been cited by a professional or regulatory governing body for disciplinary reasons?

☐ no ☐ yes (explain): _____

_____

8. What types of services do you offer?

_____

_____

9. Describe your approach to financial planning.

_____

_____

10. Will you or an associate work with me?

_____

11. If an associate will work with me or assist you, please complete questions 1–7 for the associate as well.

12. How are you paid for your services?

☐ Fee

☐ Commission (Deferred Sales Charge, Front-End Load)

☐ Fee and commission

☐ Fee offset

☐ Salary

☐ Other: _____

13. If applicable, what do you typically charge?

☐ Hourly rate: $ _____

☐ Flat fee: $ _____

☐ Percentage of assets: _____%

14. Are you affiliated with the company whose products or services you recommend?

☐ no ☐ yes (explain): _____

_____

15. Does your financial planning service include:
☐ Review of my goals and objectives?
☐ Cash management?
☐ Tax planning?
☐ Investment review?
☐ Estate planning?
☐ Insurance needs in life, disability, property/casualty?
☐ Retirement analysis?
☐ Other: _____

16. Do you provide written recommendations on my financial situation?
☐ yes (describe): _____
☐ no

17. Are the analysis and recommendations tailored to my personal needs and goals?
☐ yes (describe): _____
☐ no

18. Do you offer assistance in implementation of products?
☐ yes (describe): _____
☐ no

19. Do you offer ongoing advice regarding my financial affairs and provide regular updates on analysis or recommendations?
☐ yes (describe): _____
☐ no

20. Do you provide a written client engagement agreement?
☐ yes (describe): _____
☐ no

21. What if I feel I'm not getting my money's worth? Does

your engagement agreement provide a clause to cancel a retainer fee upon written notice?

☐ yes ☐ no

If yes, are there any penalties for doing so?

☐ no ☐ yes (describe): _____

_____

22. Does your engagement agreement include a client confidentiality clause?

☐ yes ☐ no

23. Can you provide me with a sample of your work?

☐ yes ☐ no

24. Can you provide me with the names of five people you've worked for whom I can talk to?

☐ yes ☐ no

If yes, _____

_____

_____

_____

_____

INDEX

Activities of Daily Living [ADL], 128

Action plan, 25, 36, 178-179

Adult guardianship, 89

Aerobic exercise, 41

Alcoholic beverages, 42

Alzheimer's disease, 45, 63, 137, 148

American Association of Retired People [AARP], 48, 64, 219

American Cancer Society, 214

Antioxidants, 42

Asset Marketing Systems [AMS], 304

Assisted Living Facilities, 60, 211

Baby boomers, 11, 51, 144, 218-219

Bank Accounts, 277

Bequests, 72-74, 92, 222, 229, 280

Brittle bones, 41

Business assets, 176, 231

Cancer
    breast, 215
    colon, 216
    ovarian, 217
    prostate, 216
    skin, 216
Capital
    analysis, 221, 223-224
    assets, 229
    gains, 191-192, 199-200, 223-224, 232, 254
    shortfall, 224
    surplus, 224
Car loans, 176
Car services, 55

Carbon monoxide detectors, 57

Cardiac conditions, 54, 62

Caregiver, 21, 109-113, 115, 117, 119-123, 127, 132-134, 142, 151, 156-157

Caregivers, 13, 112, 114, 116-117, 120, 122, 127, 131, 139, 142, 153, 218

Caregiving, 13, 27, 43, 75, 107, 109-111, 113-123, 125, 128, 134, 139, 150

Cash
    cash-flow shortages, 248
    legacies, 92
    management, 183-185, 193, 195, 259, 294, 296
    surplus, 241
Certificates of Deposit [CDs], 100, 155, 197, 253, 278
Charitable
    contributions, 175
    gifts, 93, 285
Chiropractor, 53
Cognitive ability, 150
    impairment, 62-63, 217, 305
Condominium, 55, 59-60, 149
Connery, Sean, 47
Conservatorship, 90
Contingent Liabilities, 176, 211
Continuing Care Retirement Community [CCRC], 59
Coronary artery bypass surgery, 264
CPAs, 240

Death benefit, 224
Debt

debt of the estate, 93
  investment, 201
  obligations, 175, 188
Dementia, 13, 40, 44-45, 75, 126,
  145-157, 217
  multiple infarct dementia, 148
Dependent
  adult children, 68
  elder, 221
Depression, 43, 76-77, 114, 126-127,
  140-141, 146, 149, 217
Dow Jones, 252
Driving, 44, 125, 137-138, 154-155
Due diligence, 201, 206-207

Eating habits, 185
Efficient Frontier, 204
Elder Connection, The, 304
Emotional abuse, 134
Employee group benefit plan, 263
Employment, 120, 175-176, 179,
  183, 186, 193, 222, 278
  benefits, 120, 176, 179
  disability benefit, 264
  full-time, 209
  income, 175, 183, 186, 193, 222,
  278
  part-time, 48
  workplace, 113, 144
Empty nester, 109
Estate
  Administration, 92
  planning, 15, 74, 172, 227-229,
  232-233, 236, 238, 240, 242-243,
  283, 294, 296
  planning checklist, 15, 232
  strategies, 167
  values, 229
Equity Index Annuities [EIA], 251-
  252

Executor, 90-91, 93, 96, 98, 104, 246,
  272-275, 277, 283-284, 288, 291

Family
  assets, 229
  business, 229
  harmony, 228, 244
  home, 55, 72-73
  law, 93-94, 232
Family and Medical Leave Act, The
  [FMLA], 119
Federal Deposit Insurance
  Corporation [FDIC], 201
  -insured, 250
Federal Housing Administration
  [FHA], 257-258
  Home Equity Conversion
  Mortgage, 257
Financial advisor, 15, 55, 81-82, 106,
  136, 162, 164, 166-168, 170, 172-
  176, 178-179, 181, 185, 187, 190,
  204-208, 221-224, 232-241, 243-
  246, 248, 261, 271, 291, 293, 295,
  297, 305
Financial planners, 237, 240, 242
  Certified Financial Planner
  [CFP], 236-238, 293, 305
  commission-based financial
  planner, 242
  fee-only financial planner, 240
  Financial Planners Standards
  Council [FPSC], 237
Financial Planning Association
  [FPA], 238
Financial Power of Attorney, 84

Food costs, 175
Formal care system, 130
  support systems, 130

Fraternal Insurance Counsellor
    [FIC], 304
Fraternal Insurance Counsellor
    Fellow [FICF], 304
Funeral home, 97, 99-105, 290
Funeral
    burial/cremation, 290
    burial vault, 98
    caskets, 97, 99
    cemetery grounds, 97
    ceremony, 100, 103
    cremation, 96-100, 102, 290
    cremation containers, 99
    earth burial, 96, 98
    expenses, 105
    graveside service, 102
    non-religious service, 103
    pre-arrangement, 104
    pre-planned funeral, 290

Geriatric care manager, 142-146
Gerontology, 79, 133, 143-144, 146,
    304-305
Government
    benefits, 183, 195, 199, 208, 278
    bond, 198
    programs, 112, 220, 222
Government senior services, 132

Hawn, Goldie, 47
Health
    benefits, 41-42, 138
    impairments, 223, 271-272, 276-
    277
Healthcare, 116, 130-131, 134, 168,
    178
    agencies, 130-131
HIV, 264
Home equity, 253-254, 257

ownership, 29
Home Equity Conversion
    Mortgage [HECM], 257-258
Home safety
    bathtub, 57
    bathroom, 55, 57, 77, 128, 154
    stove, 57, 154
Homecare, 163, 225
Home-ownership, 60
Hormonal replacement, 40
Housekeeping, 127-128, 222
    grass cutting, 128
    house cleaner, 142
Hygiene, 76, 117, 133, 136, 152
    haircuts, 54

Income plan, 251, 271
Individual Retirement Account
    [IRA], 161, 184, 190-191, 241
    IRA Investment, 190
    IRAs, 189-191, 229, 278, 281
    Traditional IRAs, 190
Informal support systems, 128-129
Insurance
    advice, 240
    companies, 95, 249, 266
    coverage, 140, 163, 210, 212,
    221, 241
    group insurance, 176
    planning, 294
    policies, 176, 278
    portfolio, 163
    products, 105
Interest income, 162, 188, 192, 197-
    200, 208, 224, 230
Internal Revenue Service [IRS], 192
Internet access, 56
Investment advisor, 181, 186, 235-
    237, 293

contrarian investment
approach, 201, 205
income, 55, 175, 183
international investments, 201
offshore trusts, 232
risk-free investment, 201
strategies, 231, 259

Kidney failure, 264

Legacies, 15, 72-74, 92, 179, 283, 286
Leisure time, 12, 48, 155
Lewy Bodies disease, 148
Life expectancy, 250
Limited Partnership Offering, 278
Lines of credit, 278
Liquidity crisis, 229
Living expenses, 183, 254
Local Community Information
Center, 132
Local senior's club, 128
Long-term care analysis, 224
facility, 63, 130, 163
disability plan, 264
insurance, 112, 211, 220, 225,
264, 278
Lymph nodes, 21

Malpractice lawsuits, 230
Managing risk, 201
stress, 43
Marital status, 271, 273
Medi-Cal, 255
Medic Alert, 153
Medical expenses, 192, 211-212
history, 216, 265
Medicare, 219, 255
Medications, 62, 127, 130, 142, 148,
217

Memory loss, 127, 141, 147, 149
Mental deterioration, 44, 148
health, 41, 43, 63, 117
Micronutrients, 42
Microwave ovens, 55
Middle age, 39, 45, 109
Military service, 272-273
Mortgages, 176, 225, 253-258, 278
Moses, Robertson, 28
MRI, 150
Multiple sclerosis, 264
Music therapists, 155
Mutual funds, 176, 245, 252, 266,
278, 294

NASDQ, 252
National Association of Securities
Dealers [NASD], 237-238
Nursing home, 63-64, 75, 140, 143-
144, 218-219

Organ donor, 288

Parkinson's disease, 40, 148
Pension
income, 175, 183, 192, 199, 249
plan, 222, 278
Personal independence, 264
liability, 212
loans, 176
records, 86
Planning fee, 167, 241-242
Police, 134-135, 139, 153
Power of Attorney, 82-86, 88-90,
134, 136
General Power of Attorney, 83
Limited Power of Attorney, 83
Medical Power of Attorney, 84
Powers of Attorney, 12, 83-84,

86, 88, 94, 123, 142, 154, 176, 227, 237, 241, 246, 283, 289
Power of Tax Deferral, 190
Prenuptial agreement, 74, 93-94, 271, 273
Private care, 220
   educational fees, 175
   healthcare agencies, 131
Probate fees, 230
   taxes, 14
Public guardian, 89
   transportation, 53, 127-128

Quality of life, 12, 40, 52, 63, 220

Real estate, 15, 58, 176, 202, 205, 208, 278
Recreational property, 174
Redford, Robert, 47
Registered Investment Advisor [RIA], 236-238, 293
Religious affiliation, 103
   communities, 96
Religious organization, 129
   Hinduism, 22
   Humanists, 104
   Judaism, 22, 96
   Unitarian, 103
Residual Beneficiaries, 286
Retirement analysis, 240, 296
   community, 32, 59
   goal, 173, 185
   home, 58, 61-62, 64, 79, 129, 132, 136, 139
   income plan, 271
   lifestyle, 175, 180
   planning, 233, 238, 258, 294, 305
   setting, 66
Reverse Mortgage, 253-258
Risk exposure, 167

management, 172, 178, 210-211, 242, 280
   tolerance, 14, 196-197, 205, 236, 248
   -free investment, 201

Safety bars, 154
   locks, 153-154
Safety Deposit Box, 291
Securities and Exchange Commission [SEC], 237-238
Self-care, 224
Senior abuse, 134
Sex, 75
Short-Term Disability, 263
Siblings, 78, 118, 120, 141, 244
Sisters of Notre Dame School, 44, 148
Sitter/companions, 133
Smoke detector, 57
Smoking, 42, 80, 214-215
Social workers, 72, 79, 130-131, 133
Society of Actuaries, 213
Spas, 95
SSI, 255
Stock market, 33, 251-252
   portfolio, 278
Strategic Life Plan, 12, 25
Subsidies, 62

Tax
   deduction, 66, 189
   liabilities, 229
   planning, 233, 294, 296
   rates, 200
   recovery, 190
Taxes, 13-14, 58, 82, 92, 95, 163, 167-169, 175-176, 178, 183, 189-190, 192, 198, 200, 208, 221-222, 224-225, 228-230, 234, 236, 241, 244, 249, 283

capital gains, 191-192, 199-200,
    223-224, 232, 254
    income taxes, 176, 200, 222, 225
    marginal tax, 165, 190, 200, 208
Tax Investment Cost, 190
T-bills, 205
Term Insurance, 223, 265
Therapists, 130-131, 155
Trust company, 87, 91, 197
Trustee, 89, 105
Turner, Tina, 47

Unexpected costs of illness, 213
Universal Life, 224, 265-267
University courses, 11
US, 11, 13-14, 44, 99, 101, 131, 165,
    192, 202-203, 205, 218, 257
    equities, 202-203
    Government, 257
U.S. Department of Housing and
    Development [HUD], 257-258
U. S. Treasury, 255

Variable Annuities, 251
Veteran, 272-273
Vitamins, 42
Volunteering, 30, 49-50, 135

Walking, 41, 44, 138, 156
Wandering, 149, 153, 156
Wheelchair, 46, 75
Will, 12, 73-75, 82, 85, 90-94, 142,
    176, 229, 231, 232-233, 237, 241,
    246
    Living will, 87-88, 288
Wrap Account, 245

X-rays, 150

Young, Edward, 171

AUTHORS

Michael S. Midlam is the President and Chief Executive Officer of Asset Marketing Systems (AMS), the largest field-marketing organization in the financial services industry. Under his direction, AMS has helped its financial advisors place in excess of $4.5 billion in fixed and equity-indexed annuity premium.

Michael has 27 years experience in both corporate and field management positions related to industry education, field training and entry-level to top financial recruitment. Before joining AMS, Michael was the Director of Management Development at a major international insurance carrier. He was accountable for the design, delivery and implementation of first and second line management skill sets that supported the company's corporate and regional business plans.

Esteemed as a creative and resourceful expert, Michael received the Purdue University Marathon Award in recognition of his achievements. He holds FIC and FICF designations and is a published author in *Life Sales* and *Broker's World Media*.

Jill L. O'Donnell, R.N., P.H.N., Cert. Social Service Administration, B.A., is the founder of Complete Geriatric Care, a private senior care consulting service established in 1981. In 1994, under the umbrella of Complete Geriatric Care, she founded *The Elder Connection,* a monthly networking breakfast. She also launched ElderMoves, a complete relocation service, in 1996. O'Donnell is a recognized pioneer in the field of gerontology, known for her work as a consultant, advocate, and educator on senior care issues, and as a lecturer and presenter at international, national, and regional conferences on aging. She has a broad knowledge of both private and public resources gained through experience in community and institutional settings. Her expertise extends to organizing treatment, and housing frail seniors who have cognitive impairment. O'Donnell is Past President of Women's College Hospital School of Nursing Alumni and is a certified registered nurse with the College of Nurses (Ontario). She is a member of the Ontario Gerontology Association.

 **Graham McWaters** works in business development for a major financial institution specializing in real-estate lending. For over nine years, he has focused on providing his services to financial advisors and their clients. In addition, McWaters has trained financial advisors in areas such as business development and lending. He also has a Bachelor of Commerce from McGill University with a major in finance and international business.

 **John A. Page,** CFP, R.F.P., is the Senior Financial Advisor at Page and Associates, Toronto, and a speaker, author, and contributor to financial advisor training programs throughout Canada. Founded in 1978, Page and Associates is recognized nationally as both a pioneer and a leading-edge provider of strategic financial planning services. Rather than manage each aspect of a client's financial world in isolation, providing tax advice, investment advice, or retirement planning, Page recognized an important truth many people

overlook—all aspects of a person's financial world are linked. Every decision an individual makes has an impact, often a profound one, on his or her long-term goals. Page founded his company of strategic financial advisors because he understood that many people don't have the time, expertise, or inclination needed to research, implement, and monitor a personal financial plan.